Alien Experiences Book Two

Evolution

Coming to Terms with the ET Presence

Nadine Lalich

HB Publishing
P. O. Box 65922
Albuquerque, NM 87193
(928) 592-5680

www.HBPublishing.net
www.AlienExperiences.com

Cover design and illustrations by Nadine Lalich

Printed in the United States of America

ISBN: 9780971177666

Contents

LIST OF ILLUSTRATIONS

ACKNOWLEDGMENTS

I want to acknowledge the following people for the many contributions they have made to the field of Ufology: Art Bell, Barbara Lamb, Betty and Barney Hill, Bob Wood, Budd Hopkins, Caroline Cory, Charles I. Halt, Coast-to-Coast Radio, David M. Jacobs Ph.D., Donald Keyhoe, Dr. Roger Leir, Eric von Daniken, George Knapp, George Noory, Gerald Clark, Giorgeio A. Tsoukalos, J. Allen Hynek, Jaime Maussan, Jim Marrs, John Greenwald, Jr., John Mack, M.D., Kathleen Marden, Leslie Kean, Linda Moulton Howe, Melinda Leslie, Mike Clelland, MUFON, Nick Pope, Paul Hellyer, Philip J. Corso, Richard Dolan, Richard H. Hall, Robert Dean, Stanton Friedman, Steve Colbern, Steven Greer, M.D., Terje Toftness, Tom DeLonge, Travis Walton, Whitley Strieber, Wilbur Allen, William J. Birnes, Yvonne Smith, and Zecharia Sitchin. I want to also acknowledge the many abductees, contactees, and experiencers who have bravely come forth to share their experiences.

INTRODUCTION

The challenging subject of UFOs has been out in the open for many years with hundreds of intelligent, analytical researchers tackling the topic. Numerous public opinion polls from the last 50 years from many countries report consistent and similar findings that approximately fifty percent of the population believes in the reality of UFOs. Today, the topic is more readily and openly discussed than ever before.

That leads us to a much bigger question: Who is driving the bus? For any of us attempting to unravel our own experiences or evaluating the enormous number of reports made about human and extraterrestrial contact, we are walking on thin ice. We must face the fact that, at best, the experiences we recall whether or not they are consciously or hypnotically retrieved are based primarily upon what we think we observed and experienced. Even the most honest and ethical person reporting an event might experience some degree of memory distortion. The previous experiences of a person, as well as their beliefs, prejudices, knowledge, and emotional state at the time an event is recorded, can alter perception. It is also commonly reported that many extraterrestrials can manipulate the human mind through various methods. Does it mean that we should disregard our memories of contact? Absolutely not! As the cosmologist, Martin Rees, succinctly put it: "Absence of evidence is not evidence of absence."[1]

---

[1] This axiom is attributed to Martin Rees, a British astrophysicist who is Astronomer Royal. It was popularized in the United States by the late Carl Sagan.

When we look back in history, we see many discoveries made by science that we once considered science fiction or nonsense. Today's scientists continue to explore many things that the human eye cannot see or that conventional technology cannot detect. The discovery of black holes is a perfect example where scientists were finally able to recognize their existence by observing how they affect and influence objects that we can see. Perhaps that would be a viable approach to take when considering the thousands of genuinely credible persons who have recollections of contact with extraterrestrials and who often manifest unexplainable psychological, emotional, and physical symptoms as a result.

The following quote from Albert Einstein regarding the universe is notable:

> ...The problem involved is too vast for our limited minds. May I not reply with a parable? The human mind, no matter how highly trained, cannot grasp the universe. We are in the position of a little child, entering a huge library whose walls are covered to the ceiling with books in many different tongues. The child knows that someone must have written those books. It does not know who or how. It does not understand the languages in which they are written. The child notes a definite plan in the arrangement of the books, a mysterious order, which it does not comprehend, but only dimly suspects. We see a universe marvelously arranged, obeying certain laws, but we understand the laws only dimly. Our limited minds cannot grasp the mysterious force that sways the constellations.[2]

---

[2] Albert Einstein, as cited in George Sylvester Viereck, *Glimpses of the Great*, The Macaulay Company, (1930)

One reason for mainstream science's refusal to take the ET abduction phenomenon seriously is the fact that the number of witnesses held in high esteem are limited. Those people would be more highly educated and in recognized positions of power and prominence such as science, academia, government, law enforcement, or military. Such people, so often referred to as trained observers, might positively promote greater interest in the phenomenon, but it is these very people who due to fear of the consequences to their reputation and career who are the most reluctant to speak out.

Let us consider the average citizen who has what he or she believes to be a contact with a non-terrestrial. Unfortunately, not everyone can express themselves in what might be considered a restrained and logical manner, especially with the heavily charged emotions are involved as often happens with the ET contact phenomenon. In my case, when I first began to speak about the subject at a public level, I was quite emotionally charged. I was not nearly as capable of expressing myself as well as I do fifteen years later. Yet, manner of expression should not invalidate an experiencer's claims of ET contact. If more experiencers were to present their encounters from an analytical, systematic point of view, their statements and the subject at large would undoubtedly attract more considerable positive attention and respect. In this way, the number of credible people reporting the experiences would increase, and the entire UFO and ET phenomenon would be considered more worthy of investigation.

In most cases, events like those included in this book can be disturbing and traumatic for the experiencer. Those who have endured the bizarre phenomenon and are brave enough to speak about their experience must suffer further insult through ridicule and potential damage to their reputation amongst family, friends, and colleagues. Most often, it is the experiencer's initial desire to stop the intrusion, which eventually leads them to investigate and speak about their experiences. Fortunately, over time if the fear can dissipate, the experiencer may achieve a degree of resolution and find an open doorway into a new or expanded view of the nature of reality and God.

Evolution: Coming to Terms with the ET Presence has been a long time coming because I also feared repercussions in my work and personal life. Since retiring from the legal field, I am much less concerned about discussing the subject in public. I have also come to understand the significance of the information derived from UFO and ET investigation and the impact it will have upon the survival of humanity and the earth. Although the ambiguous details derived from abductee testimony can be difficult to explain and categorize, these reports deserve consideration simply because, theoretically, these experiencers may have actually been in direct contact with extraterrestrial or interdimensional life. Should that be proven true, such knowledge could dramatically impact the evolution of human consciousness.

The majority of the events I have depicted in this book were consciously recalled. Also included are excerpts from several hypnotic regressions conducted by Barbara Lamb, MS, MFT, CHP, and Yvonne Smith, CHT. Collectively, it covers my personal UFO, ET, and MILAB experiences from childhood up to 2010.

It is important to note that after my first meeting with Barbara Lamb in 2005, it took another year or so before I felt comfortable enough to look at other cases. During that time, I kept the focus on reviewing and transcribing my own experiences from the dozens of journals I had accumulated over the years. I did not want to color my recollections in any way.

I recognize that perception is subjective, memory imperfect, and that alternative explanations may exist to define some of this phenomenon you will read about. However, I can state, unequivocally, that I have presented the events and information honestly and to the best of my ability as it was stored in my memory. I have not deliberately embellished nor manipulated the material.

Until more conclusive information can be collected, this aspect of my life remains inclusive and a fascinating mystery. The subject is certainly worthy of pursuit; therefore, I will continue to explore and investigate. Undoubtedly, my hypothesis will grow, but at this point, I do believe we are not alone in the universe. I also believe that extraterrestrial beings most probably have been and will continue to be in contact with us in some manner.

If we hope to solve the multitude of crises facing our planet, we will need to break the chains of military and political corruption. To do so will require that we open ourselves to the truth that we live in a far grander, more intelligent, and expansive reality than we ever dreamed. To bring this fascinating and mystifying subject to the forefront of human consciousness could assist our survival and promote our evolution as universal citizens.

1
A BRIEF HISTORY

There is a great deal of evidence that indicates UFOs and non-human entities have been interacting with the earth and humans throughout history for thousands of years. Ancient petroglyphs and 14th to 18th-century paintings from across the globe depict non-human beings and aerial crafts interacting with humans. In the 1940s, the number of reports began to increase with an even more dramatic escalation in number after the development and use of atomic energy. In present times thousands of credible stories of UFO encounters, many with substantial verifying evidence, have been made by intelligent people from all walks of life, including high-ranking military personal from all branches of service.

The non-human beings encountered or observed by people worldwide have generally been referred to as extraterrestrials, ETs, or aliens, implying that they are physical beings not originating from the earth. More recently, researchers have termed a different type of being that may reside and travel in dimensions other than our third dimension, referred to as interdimensional beings.

According to some polls, the observation of unidentified flying crafts is a worldwide phenomenon involving as many as eight million people in the United States alone. As a result of the "Phoenix Lights" incident that was observed by thousands of people on March 13, 1997, 20th Century Fox Home Entertainment, before the release of its movie, "Phoenix Forgotten," commissioned a survey as part of their promotional campaign for which 1,700 Americans responded as follows:

> The survey reported that 47 percent of Americans believe in aliens, which is about 150 million people. That number is up 5 percent from the 2012 survey commissioned by National Geographic. Unfortunately, the survey didn't measure those who are on the fence about the existence of aliens or the percentage who flat out don't believe they exist.
>
> The survey reported that 38.78 percent of Americans believe aliens have visited Earth before, which is around 124 million Americans. It also reported that 16.74 percent say they have seen a UFO. This indicates that 53.57 million Americans say they have seen a UFO; that's 1 in 6 Americans. The old rule-of-thumb estimate was around 1 in 10.[3]

Abductions are reported taking place at any time of the day or night, although a commonly reported time is between 11:00 p.m. and 5:00 a.m. Abductions can take place when people are in their beds, inside automobiles on rural

---

[3] Cheryl Costa, "UFOs, Aliens and Abductions Survey," Syracuse Newstimes, (2017) Accessed October 3, 2019, https://www.syracusenewtimes.com/ufos-aliens-and-abductions-survey.

highways, or late at night. In a group situation, only one person may be abducted while the remaining people are rendered in an unconscious or semi-unconscious state until after the abductee returns. Abductions can also take place in broad daylight from within a building or on open ground, with other people in the area who may or may not notice the event.

People appear to be abducted by extraterrestrials for a variety of reasons that include medical examinations and retrieval of eggs and semen, theoretically to promote a hybrid species and for monitoring human activity. Surgically implanting devices into abductees have also been often reported with some suggested reasons being to record body functions, for tracking purposes, or to monitor mental and emotional states. Implants may also serve to stimulate activity or responses in the person implanted or download or retrieve information from the brain. Other reasons include human interaction with hybrid offspring.

Alien abductions and examinations appear to be genetically driven, targeting all persons within an entire family from one generation to the next. It usually begins in childhood and continues throughout adulthood. Many female abductees have reported memories of being implanted with a hybrid fetus and having a positive pregnancy confirmation, only to later have the pregnancy and the fetus disappear. Months later, these same females might be taken aboard a craft and encouraged to interact with an unusual looking baby whom they feel incredibly drawn to and sometimes believe it may be their child. They are urged to hold and bond with the strange, frail babies who do not look entirely human. Often abductees find themselves in large nurseries where many children with severely mal-formed bodies are kept.

Some abductees report collaborating with aliens during abductions and acting as a liaison between ETs and human abductees. They have reported assisting with medical procedures and co-piloting crafts through a form of telepathy. Others have memories of attending what appear to be large meetings comprised of multiple species of aliens.

Most abductees initially experience a great deal of fear and turmoil from the bizarre experiences, but over time with investigation and support, many find a resolution. Those who suffer the more malevolent species have greater difficulty moving past the fear and integrating the phenomenon into their lives. Regardless of the nature of the contacts and the species involved, if the abductee becomes committed to a resolution, they can successfully process and reframe the experience of contact in a way that will allow them to release the fear. In doing so, the survival of humanity and the earth often becomes significantly more meaningful, and motivations and goals can shift in that direction. Concepts of the cosmos, the nature of consciousness, and even life and death issues can change dramatically in a positive way. Compassion for all living beings and a dedication to service can also develop, leading to a stronger spiritual path.

The Abduction Scenario

Typical abductions appear to take place as a physical experience often during the night when people are lying in bed asleep or awake. Many can take place during the daytime when the person is fully awake and conscious, via lucid dreaming or during deep meditation. In most cases, the captors employ a technique that paralyzes the abductee, ostensibly to give them more control of the situation. There is also a theory that the paralysis may help to enable the particles of a body to separate more easily to allow movement through a solid wall or closed window. The unforeseen and intrusive quality of an abduction allows the abductee no room for choice, thus creating an abuser/victim scenario. A physical abduction is often verified when the abductee subsequently finds strange markings on his or her body or other physical indications that the body was affected.

Another type of encounter reported suggests that the extraterrestrials use some form of technology to remove the consciousness or energy body from a person while leaving their physical body behind. During such an astral or out-of-body experience, the abductee's psyche is taken and later returned to their body, sometimes with a person being fully aware and seeing their physical body left behind. Other abductions appear to be a combination of physical and astral events.

Varieties of Beings

According to reports from thousands of people worldwide, there are many different types of aliens, and, over time, an abductee may encounter a variety of species often during one abduction. They can be tall or short, with or without hair, insensitive or compassionate. The following is only a partial representation of alien species reported worldwide.

The most common type of being described by abductees is the Grey, who is three to four feet tall with grey skin and large solid black, almond-shaped eyes. The smooth, hairless head is large and out-of-proportion for the small, slender body which resembles a child. The nose is barely discernable, the mouth a small slit, and the chin pointed. They behave robotically and emotionless with no regard for the abductee's reactions. Another species of Grey look quite similar, but are taller and act less robotically. These beings, referred to as Tall Greys, often conduct what is referred to as a mind scan by staring into an abductee's eyes close to the face. One theory suggests that they may be accessing the abductee's thoughts and memories, or programming their brain in some fashion. To the person experiencing a mind scan, it is a startling, invasive, and frightening experience.

Similar in appearance to the Tall Greys are the extraterrestrials referred to as Little Whites, named for their intensely white, chalky-colored skin. Their eyes are more rounded and display a small amount of white sclera. They are more interactive and responsive to humans and less threatening than the Greys, but also conduct abductions and, medical procedures in the abductee's home or on a craft.

One species that is quite disturbing to many experiencers stands at least six feet with muscular physiques and possessing many of the characteristics of a reptile. This race is called Reptilian, and both male and female genders have been present. A Reptilian's demeanor is commanding and aggressive, suggesting a warrior-like persona, and they wear chest armor, banners with emblems, or sometimes capes or robes. There have been reports of violent behavior toward humans and, on occasion, to engage in sexual relations with human members of the opposite sex. The names Dracos or Draconians have been used to describe similar lizard-like beings who may or may not be the same species as the Reptilian species.

Another commonly described alien species is referred to as Insectoids because they resemble a praying mantis. Although potentially repellant from a human perspective, many who have encountered these species find them to be benevolent, and some abductees develop a fondness for them.

There are other aliens referred to as Hybrids who are genetically engineered, conceivably through combining human and alien reproductive material. From a distance, they can appear reasonably human, but closer contact reveals they are not. Their eyes are quite similar but larger than a human, and they are usually emotionally detached and non-responsive. Allegedly, some Hybrids look human enough to be able to intermingle with humans on Earth without detection.

Several other types of light-skinned beings reported include a very-human-looking blonde Nordic race, the Tall Whites who oversee and supervise examinations, and a race well over six feet with wispy hair and a skull-like face. The Sasquatch or Big Foot race often reported in the United States is similar to an enormous ape and may actually be an alien or interdimensional race. There have also been reports of a Goblin or Elf race that is four feet tall with pointed ears and sharp, pointed teeth.

Finally, well-publicized beings referred to as Men in Black are known to contact UFO investigators or abductees in their homes or offices. They often confiscate material evidence related to alien activity, alien technology, or human governmental involvement with aliens and abductees. The Men in Black exhibit robot-like manners suggesting they may be androids. These entities generally dress in black suits and hats, often fashioned after the 1940 era styles, wear sunglasses and speak in a monotone, canned voice. They are demanding and sometimes threatening, but their energy tends to deplete quickly. Therefore, the visitations are generally short-lived, and as they depart, they have been observed staggering and sometimes disappearing into thin air after a short distance. They have been seen to arrive in large, black 1940-1950 era sedans which have can vanish instantly. These beings could be an alien race, Hybrids, or androids.

In general, although there is rarely any apparent indication of gender, abductees do tend to identify extraterrestrials as male or female by their demeanor and by the vibrations they emit.

Alien Behavior

Many of the aliens described herein appear to work together cooperatively during the abduction of humans. Certain species initiate the abduction, removing the abductee from his home or other location, and transferring him to a craft. Others perform medical procedures on the abductee while he is lying on an examining table, while another species sometimes perform a mind scan by visually penetrating the abductee's eyes close to his face. Often, a being is near the abductee, apparently to calm and comfort by touching various parts of the human body, such as his forehead, shoulder, arms, or wrist. A leader is often present who simply observes the examinations from the background and often has been a Tall White. Also, there are reports of aliens who conduct complicated procedures on the abductee in an attempt to promote physical healing.

Medical procedures commonly take place, often involving the reproductive organs. Sometimes an abductee is also provided instruction in reading star maps, healing techniques, or is encouraged to learn alien symbols or writing. Abductees are also often shown devastating holographic scenes of Earth that portray nuclear destruction, massive earthquakes, or other catastrophic views. Provocative staged events are produced on a screen or possibly projected into the abductee's mind to trigger an emotional response. Such staged scenarios that are closely observed by the extraterrestrials might include seeing a child being struck by a car, having a deceased loved one or a current lover suddenly appear, or seeing a horrific action perpetrated upon a fellow human. The following are some additional observations made about the behavior and abilities of various extraterrestrials:

According to the researcher and psychotherapist, Barbara Lamb, over 50 different alien species have been reported in her recorded cases. Some ET races appear to be solely self-serving, somewhat threatening with minimal regard for humans, while others seem relatively benign and non-threatening. There are also reports of interactions with several other races that have been quite positive, with the extraterrestrials being sincerely interested in supporting humanity.

Extraterrestrials can control what we think we see. Some species appear to be able to shapeshift and can appear to us in any number of guises, perhaps through altering an abductee's brain and perception. They may have the ability to render themselves partially or fully invisible and can remove human consciousness from a physical body.

After ET contact, abductees report many different effects left on their skin, including scoop marks, straight-line scars, singular punctures, or multiple puncture wounds in a triangle shape. Bruises and three-fingered indentations are also common. Some races demonstrate a profound interest in human sexuality and reproduction, causing female abductees to suffer gynecological problems later, including endometriosis and missing fetuses.

Abductees often recall being instructed and trained by aliens using various equipment. This training may be in the form of verbal or telepathic lessons, slide shows, or actual hands-on instruction in the operation of alien technology.

Abductees report being taken to facilities where they encounter not only aliens but also normal-looking humans, sometimes in military uniforms, working with the alien captors. Abductees often encounter more than one type of alien during an experience. They report seeing nurseries filled with hybrid, genetically modified babies and rooms housing containers of humanoid fetuses.

Aliens make predictions of an imminent period of global chaos and destruction. They say that a certain number of humans will be rescued from the planet to continue the species, either on another planet or back on Earth. According to noted Harvard Psychiatrist, Dr. John Mack, abductions last from the cradle to the grave. Age, social status, income, occupation, and lifestyle are no deterrent to being taken. Some people are aware that abduction is a phenomenon taking place in their life, and they may have conscious memories or not. Other people may be utterly unaware of part or, potentially, all of their life.

Response to an abduction event can vary widely depending upon a person's personality, ranging from terror to feeling special for having been chosen. Women tend to stress the emotional aspects of the experience with feelings of being abused, while men tend to respond more physically with anger. A sense of loss of control and the reality of being defenseless can be overwhelming for many.

The Skeptic and the Believer

In the case of UFOs ("Unidentified Flying Objects") or UAPs ("Unidentified Aerial Phenomenon"), as they are sometimes now referred to, there is a massive amount of information and evidence available today to substantiate their existence. That evidence includes credible witness testimonies, government documentation, expertly analyzed videos and photos, and electromagnetic, radar and radioactivity anomalies. On the other hand, outside of witness testimony, concrete evidence to substantiate the abduction of humans by extraterrestrials is extremely rare. Indeed, some worldwide phenomenon is taking place (with myself included), but the limited scientific evidence available makes the exact nature of these experiences challenging to determine. An intriguing possibility for developing more definitive proof of human and alien contact is the late Dr. Roger Leir's research into alleged alien implants.

Generally, most people consider themselves to be either a believer or a skeptic because it tends to make us feel more comfortable and in control. But labels can also lock us in and limit our ability to contemplate new information that we may consider outside of what we consider normal or possible. Perhaps we who are researching this fascinating phenomenon might better serve ourselves and the investigation at large by working harder to refrain from making concrete conclusions prematurely. It is not an easy task to remain more neutral, especially for those of us who are entrenched in the contact phenomenon, but to do so will assist us as we evaluate future information.

Other than for a claim of lack of evidence, what different motivations might there be for a skeptical person or government to debunk, cover-up, or spread disinformation about UFOs and ETs? Reasons might include conscious or unconscious apprehension and fear of personal harm or a change of status or loss of power. In our current human condition and our society-at-large, openly declaring that we are not alone in the universe would shatter long-held beliefs and cause us all to rethink the power, influence, and control that granted to religion, politics, and corporations. Worldwide, our human perspective would need to be reviewed, drastically adjusted, and a new agenda drawn for the future.

We have often heard it said that believers or those claiming ET contact might be seeking attention, monetary gain, or perhaps may even be suffering from mental or emotional dysfunction. No doubt, some people may be attention seekers and those who have emotional or psychological issues, but rarely do they gain the favor they seek. On the other hand, the majority of experiencers and researchers are ordinary people dealing with extraordinary circumstances who must learn to incorporate the phenomenon into their daily lives. For them to openly investigate and speak about their strange experiences is to take the road less traveled, a path fraught with prejudice and risk. Rarely do they find their family, colleagues, or friends open to discussing the subject, and if they do talk about their experiences, ridicule, rejection, and a loss of reputation often result. Overall, revealing these experiences to others can create a negative impact that often outweighs any personal gain achieved. For those reasons alone, there are untold numbers of viable witnesses with valuable information about UFOs and extraterrestrial life that may never come forward.

As for most of the media and those declared skeptics of the UFO and ET phenomena, they do gain a great deal more positive personal attention. With little risk to reputation or relationships, they take the stand before the public as being more intelligent, logical, and in control than the investigator or those who have paranormal experiences. Often these proclaimed skeptics have little knowledge of the subject, yet they write and sell books, give interviews and speak at conferences, garnering more positive results and mainstream media attention.

It requires vigilance to maintain a rational perspective and an open, curious mind when investigating the considerable volume of material available on this subject. It is also good to remember that most of what science knows today was at one time considered impossible. When evaluating data, we should also take into consideration the possible agendas of other people, organizations, and even ourselves. An investigation is at its best when we work without fear and avoid preconceived judgment as much as possible. To do so can make exploring the life and mysteries of the universe a fascinating journey of infinite discovery.

2
THE AWAKENING

One of the most extraordinary events of my life occurred on June 15, 1991, approximately 20 miles north of downtown Sedona, Arizona. Having driven all day from California with my friend, Pamela, we were exhausted and decided to stop for the night before heading the next morning to the vortexes of Sedona for a hiking adventure. We had been driving south on 89A in the moonless, and pitch-black night when we pulled into the first site we found - Banjo Bill Park in Oak Creek Canyon. It was a daytime picnic spot with ten or twelve small clearings, each with a table and fire grill. There was no electricity or other services available, just a rustic restroom. Other than the two of us, the park was deserted. The only sound we could hear was the wind in the trees, and the water moving through Oak Creek. There was no lighting other than a single light near the toilets at the end of the dirt parking lot, so we relied upon our flashlights to set up our camp. After building a small fire in the metal grill, we sat talking under the stars until about 11:00 p.m. During the entire time, I had the uncomfortable feeling that someone was watching us.

©2020 Nadine Lalich

Road to Sedona

©2020 Nadine Lalich

Overnight Camp

Before retiring, we emptied the van of all our camping equipment and personal belongings, setting everything on the picnic table located toward the end of the vehicle. Those items included an ice chest, lantern, chairs, food, and our clothing and toiletries. We were sleeping soundly in our sleeping bags when, sometime after midnight, I was awakened by noises outside of the van. It sounded as if several people were walking alongside the vehicle. Concerned about being in an isolated area, I sat up quickly, straining to hear more clearly. Four or five seconds later, the back door of the van abruptly swung open, activating the interior lights and temporarily blinding me. It took a few more seconds for my vision to adjust when I saw a long, thin, grey arm and hand with three fingers and a thumb reaching toward me. The tip of each of the fingers appeared to be indented as if to create a suction cup.

Terror and adrenaline shot through me, and I momentarily lost consciousness. The next thing I knew, I was standing outside at the end of the van with the open overhead door illuminating the immediate area around me. I believe I lost less than a minute.

As I stood there, my body felt stiff, and my arms hung straight along my sides. I was completely paralyzed and unable to move. My chin felt forcefully tucked to my chest, limiting my ability to raise my head. The only area that I could directly see was from my shoulders to the ground, with a circumference of perhaps ten feet. At the time, I did not know about the Greys; therefore, I believed what I was seeing was two bald children with large heads, standing three or four feet tall, one on each side of me. I could not see, but also sensed a much taller and more powerful presence standing there.

Suddenly, my bare feet rose off the ground several inches, and I noted that the children had placed their cupped hands directly beneath mine, but not touching. We began to move slowly forward, and I could see the ground passing beneath my feet. Off to the side, but still within my circumference of vision, I could see other little children surrounding us and following. Frantically trying to analyze the situation, I knew the beings were not children, but it served to calm my hysteria. As we continued along, I saw the ground beneath my feet grow lighter from what I surmised to be an extremely bright light ahead of us. Several times I also felt something brush across my face, but it held little interest for me compared to my fear of our destination. I lost consciousness at that point.

Sometime later, I regained consciousness and felt myself being dropped back into the van in a manner that suggested I entered directly through the vehicle's roof! I even bounced slightly as I fell onto the top of my sleeping bag. Immediately looking at my watch, I saw that it was 3:30 a.m. Terrified and desperately trying to reason with myself, I could not shake the feeling that what had just happened was real. More than that, I was obsessed with the thought that they were coming back and going to perform experiments on me. Panic-stricken, I aggressively tried to wake up Pamela, yelling and shaking her, but she remained unresponsive in a deep sleep. At that point in my life, I had no memory of ever experiencing anything similar to that event. It would be years before I would fully recall and accept the fact that the ET phenomenon truly began in my very early years.

©2020 Nadine Lalich

Hovering Craft and Occupants

©2020 Nadine Lalich

Transported by Greys to Craft

2013 Photograph of Area where Craft Landed in 1991

For the next two hours, I remained awake and vigilant with my face pressed to the back window of the van. At about 5:30 a.m.., as it was beginning to get light, Pamela suddenly awoke and we exited the vehicle. I shared only brief comments about my experience, as I found talking about it difficult. She attentively listened as we had coffee sitting at the picnic table. Our camp and supplies appeared untouched, but we soon realized that all of my personal belongings that had been left outside were gone. Repeated searching of the surrounding area proved unfruitful; my bag, with clothing, shoes and towel inside were gone. Knowing how ridiculous it sounded, I nonetheless tried to reassure myself that an animal must have taken my things.

I was quite disturbed by the incident, unable to shake off my fear, so we packed up and left the area shortly after that. Although we mentioned the bizarre incident briefly several times during our long drive back to California, I mostly wanted to forget what had happened.

Over the next six months, I became strangely obsessed with moving to Santa Fe, New Mexico, and finally purchased an airline ticket to explore the area. Although I had not secured employment, and I knew no one in the state, I nonetheless felt compelled to move there in January of 1992. I rented a house in a somewhat remote area, and, rather than escaping the phenomenon, the move triggered more frequent events encompassing a greater variety of elements. Three or four times each week, I would experience what I considered a physical contact, or I would have prolific, detailed dreams of ET contact. I would sometimes awake suddenly in the middle of the night and sense that they were outside of my bedroom window, and sometimes I would actually wake to see one in my room standing at the foot of the bed. I would see strange lights in the sky and hear odd buzzing sounds while at home alone in the middle of the day.

There were times when I was fully awake and moving about in the house that I would become so tired I would sit down and suddenly lose consciousness. An hour or two later, I would awake in an odd position or location, confused and wondering what had happened. I soon developed a host of what I considered to be irrational fears, checking behind doors, in closets, or the back seat of my car, always driven by an uneasy feeling that someone might be hiding there. Periodically, I experienced bleeding from my nose or ears during the nighttime. There were frightening, lucid nightmares of extraterrestrials, examination tables, and memories of being on space crafts. All the while I struggled to understand what was happening to me, I refused to reach out and investigate the matter in any way. I kept the secret to myself and began a journal to record each occurrence, determined to believe an alternate explanation existed. Deep within, however, I knew the events were based in reality.

Later that year, I decided to see a therapist in Santa Fe. I refrained from telling her what had happened, only that something unusual had transpired that evening in Sedona, and it was continuing to cause me distress. She was able to easily hypnotize me into a deep state of mind on two occasions. Both times I was able to recall more than just the beginning and end of the event. I remembered more details about our movement through the forest, such as the fact that tree branches were hitting my face. I also had a much better recollection of the disk-shaped craft where I was taken and the ET species that were involved. It was odd that from the outside, the ship appeared to be 25-30 feet in diameter, but once I was inside, it seemed a great deal larger. I also remembered being forced to lay naked upon a metal examining table. At this point, during both hypnotic regressions, my emotions escalated to the point that the therapist terminated the session to calm me.

I recalled one other aspect of the encounter. I was standing in a large room alone when I noticed an opening into another area. I stepped to look through the doorway and saw what looked like other human beings lying down in rows of flat containers as if they were sleeping. I remembered someone pulling me away from the area, and my next awareness was of being physically dropped with a big swooshing sound of air, and I bounced onto my sleeping bag wide awake and sitting upright.

Over the years, the events continued and included variations of the abduction scenario involving different species. I began a journal that I kept on my nightstand so that I would be able to record any paranormal activity that occurred immediately. My journal offered great relief by providing an outlet for my frustration, and a place where I could meticulously record the details and make sketches of the abductions right after they occurred. Most often, they happened in the middle of the night, and immediately afterward, I would often write for an hour or more. As the years passed, I had accumulated a great deal of information but continued to refrain from openly discussing the subject with anyone other than Pamela. I still hoped I might find an alternative answer to the phenomena.

On January 12, 2004, my mother suddenly passed away. Her death drew attention, which ushered in another active period of abductions that motivated me to take some action for relief. I did some research and found out about the organization, the Mutual UFO Network ("MUFON"), which held regular monthly meetings in Orange County, California, not far from where I lived. I attended my first meeting in 2004, and found out that a world of experiencers and researchers of UFOs and ET abduction had existed for decades! Eventually, I was directed to a psychotherapist and researcher, Barbara Lamb, whom I met in January 2005. For the first time, I was able to describe in detail my experience of that first night to another person, during which time I cried and raged indignantly.

The following is an excerpt from a May 5, 2005, transcript from a hypnotic regression conducted by Barbara Lamb regarding the incident.

BL: We are now back in the year of 1991, and it's June 15th. You and your friend have gone to Sedona, Arizona. After driving for many hours, it's getting late, and you decided to pull off the road into a campground for the night, and you went to sleep in the van. Tell me what happened then.

NL: We were sleeping. They opened up the back door and took me out.

BL: And probably the van was locked, I would imagine?

NL: Yes. I felt it coming before it even happened that night. I had a dream one month before we went. Then I needed to go to Sedona.

BL: So, you are sleeping in the van with Pamela, mid-June 1991, in Sedona, Arizona.

NL: I'm sleeping on a pad. It's warm inside, but cold outside now.

BL: What position are you sleeping in?

NL: I'm on my back.

BL: At this moment that you are reliving, is Pamela in the van with you?

NL: Yes.

BL: And does it seem like she is sleeping, too?

NL: Yes.

BL: Okay. So, you're sleeping on your back in the van. What are you aware of now?

NL: I hear shuffling sounds outside.

BL: Does it sound like the sound is coming from down toward the ground or is higher?

NL: It's right where I am.

BL: Is it coming from just one side of the van or all around?

NL: I don't know.

BL: And as you hear the shuffling sounds, are you thinking about what that might be?

NL: I am concerned, but I just want to sleep.

BL: Even if you are falling asleep, a part of you that can be aware of the shuffling sounds. Just notice them. Your mind is aware and has recorded everything that has happened even when your body is asleep. We are allowing that to come forth now, the awareness of the shuffling. Notice if it seems to be in just one small area or if it's more extensive than that.

NL: It has scattered around me outside and around the end of the van.

BL: Just let this experience continue now. You hear the shuffling and notice if something else seems to happen.

NL: I hear a click on the back door, and the door swings up, way high. The light is on now, too.

BL: The van light inside?

NL: Yes, the lights go on when the back door swings up.

BL: So the light is on. Is it dark outside?

NL: Yes, it's dark.

BL: So, you are lying there on your back.

NL: I'm not on my back. I sat up.

BL: And your eyes opened?

NL: Oh, yes! This is freaky. This has never happened before!

BL: So you see the light on and the darkness outside. Is the back door of the van all the way open now?

NL: Yes. The three fingers are awful. It has three long, skinny fingers, a skinny arm, and it's reaching in the van towards me. They have little pads or cups at the end of the finger. It's a weird color, kind of a grey-green.

BL: The skins of these fingers are grey?

NL: Yes.

BL: Do you see what those three fingers are attached to?

NL: No, not right away, I don't. I just see the hand, and I don't ever remember seeing anything like it before. It wants to pull me outside.

BL: Has it touched you at this point?

NL: It must have touched me because I'm out of the van, but I don't remember getting out. The door is wide open, and I'm standing on the ground in my nightgown. I'm terrified.

BL: So you are standing on the ground now, and you're terrified. Can you notice if anybody else is there with you?

NL: I'm barefoot, and there's dirt, little pebbles on my feet underneath. I feel frozen, and I can't move at all. I'm paralyzed!

BL: And yet you are upright?

NL: Yes, I'm upright and standing.

BL: Is anything propping you up?

NL: No. I'm just standing up straight, and no one is touching me. There is a little taller one in front of me and three shorter ones on each side, but they're not touching me. They're just holding their hands underneath mine, cupping them, but not touching me. They make me rise off the ground a few inches. I can't move! It's like being tied up. You can't move at all!

BL: So you are not high off the ground?

NL: No. I'm just an inch or two off the ground. I'm surprised I'm not cold.

BL: Oh, I'm surprised too. Now, the one you mentioned who is in front, can you get a look at this one?

NL: I don't remember him like this before, but he's taller, definitely bigger. The others are little, something like three and a half feet tall. This one is five feet tall, at least, maybe even taller. He's not like the others.

BL: When you say he is not like him, does he have a different kind of head and face?

NL: It's angular. He is more double-jointed or something and brown. It's as if all the others serve this one.

BL: What about his eyes distinctly? What are they like?

NL: His head is different. Wow! It's as if they work together. I thought he was a grey one like the others, but he is not like that at all.

BL: Is he with the little grey ones?

NL: Yes, he is.

BL: Okay. Well, that's interesting to know. These different species do seem to collaborate.

NL: He is guiding the way, telling them where to go and how to do it, and they follow him. They're just like little automatons. I thought at first that there was just them and us, but there's a lot of more of the little ones around us just watching. I can see a face in the bushes watching.

BL: And are they like the little ones who were around you?

NL: Yes, They're small, with big heads, forehead, and big eyes. This guy in front is gross! I don't know what he is. I think he made himself look like the others at first.

BL: What about his body?

NL: His skin is rough and wrinkled. There is some kind of armor over his chest. It looks like it's an external armor attached to his body. I don't get this at all! The way he walks is weird as though his legs and joints are facing backward.

BL: What else is he wearing besides that plate of armor? Does he have any other clothes on that you can see?

NL: Where the joints are, it's knobby. He might be wearing something like the armor on his legs, too.

BL: So when you think of the joints, you think of elbows?

NL: His knee seems like it's backward. Gross!

BL: What about his sense of weight? Is he heavy, medium, or light?

NL: He's bulgy in spots where the joints meet, but more slender on the sides. He's ugly, not like the others. The others are not ugly, and there is nothing really to see. This one is ugly!

BL: And what do you sense about this one?

NL: He is in charge, guiding and directing the thing. It doesn't seem like they think for themselves. I'm glad I'm calm. I can't feel the terror now.

BL: Has anything like this ever happened before?

NL: No.

BL: Have you seen these little ones before?

NL: At home, when I was little.

BL: Okay, so there is something familiar about them that you are experiencing right now in Sedona.

NL: Yes.

BL: This taller one who is so different looking, is he familiar in any way? Do you think you have ever seen him or one like him before this experience in Sedona?

NL: I don't know. He's a warrior, a fighter. The others are smooth, and they're not conscious. This guy is much more powerful, but he is not like the guy on the ship. The guy on the ship was tall and pasty-white color.

BL: What about his shoulders? Can you see his shoulders?

NL: He is bigger on the top and smaller on the bottom.

BL: Okay, so he has broad shoulders?

NL: Yes. He could be as much as six feet. His skin is so bumpy, with ridges and rough looking.

BL: What do his hands and fingers look like?

NL: He is much more aggressive, and he feels everything, and there's some kind of odor.

BL: Just notice that now.

NL: Yes, there's some odor, and I think he is playing

himself down, so he doesn't look so threatening or so big. He seems to be curious about me. He's directing us toward a big white glow in the woods. You can see it in between the trees. They don't touch me, just put their hands under my hand, and it lifts me.

BL: They don't pick you up or anything?

NL: Nobody is touching me, but they're still moving me.

BL: So, to move you, all they do is gently touch your hands?

NL: No, they're not actually touching my hands, just putting theirs underneath. They cup their hand underneath mine, and it raises me a couple of inches.

BL: Are the little ones doing this?

NL: Yes. They're moving me away from the van.

BL: And as you are moving away from the van, is the back door of the van still up and the light on and everything?

NL: I can't see behind me. I'm moving forward.

BL: Okay. Are you seeing the woods ahead of you, or are the woods all around you anyway?

NL: We're in the clearing where we were camped, and now I'm just scooting across the ground. The tree branches are hitting my face, and I can see this white light ahead of me. It's so bright on my eyes!

BL: Are you still upright?

NL: Yes, I am standing straight up. I don't know where the other guy has gone. Now we're in another clearing, and the white light is so bright. I feel lots of presence around me, although I'm not seeing them right now. I'm feeling so detached from my feelings, but I think this is the scariest thing that ever happened to me in my life!

BL: Yes, because you have no idea what's going to happen?

BL: What is happening now?

NL: I don't know where the other guy has gone. Now we're in another clearing, and the white light is so bright.

BL: And what do you see with that brightness?

NL: The light looks misty now, not so bright anymore, just a fading mist. I see metal, and it looks like brushed stainless steel. You can't see anything on the metal, and then I see a crack all of a sudden. It wasn't there, and then this crack opens up, and it slides apart so you can go in.

BL: Have you been able to see the shape of this thing?

NL: I only saw a piece of it, a soldered edge where it comes down. It's definitely like a saucer and round. I can see it going around. It has to be much bigger than what I can see. It has to be a hundred feet across. It's huge!

BL: Is it shiny at all?

NL: It's not shiny, more like a dull, brushed stainless steel and silver grey.

BL: And then suddenly it opens up?

NL: It does, and I'm moving in. I don't want to go in!

BL: Are you moving in?

NL: Yes, and I see a guy on the other side of the room. I don't like him. He turned and looked at me. He is really tall, maybe seven feet tall and skinny wearing some long coat or cape. Oh, I mean nothing to him!

BL: Is he anything like that taller one who was with you outside, or is he different?

NL: No. He's different — this one's pale, pasty-white, much straighter, and smoother.

BL: Do you mean straight upright posture?

NL: He has weird eyes, too. There is an instrument panel in front of him. The ceiling comes down to the bottom of the room, and there's an instrument panel there, too. There are lots of different things in that center section.

BL: Can you notice anything about the instrument area there?

NL: In front of him is an examining table that reminds me of a slab at a morgue. I know I'm going to end up on that table!

BL: Do you know you are going to end up on it?

NL: Yes.

BL: Does any of this seem familiar at all, like you've been in this kind of a room with these unusual beings and seeing that table and being on that table ever? Does it ring a bell?

NL: When I was small, maybe five years old.

BL: Do you remember from way back, years ago?

NL: I know they hold your wrist, and then somebody is assigned to you just to keep you calm. Their whole concentration is just to keep you calm. They do something with pressure points on your wrist, too.

BL: So it's a specific way of holding your wrist?

NL: Oh, yes!

BL: Are you feeling upset now?

NL: This is just not good because this is all sexual. It's a terrible thing to do that to me, to hold me down and touch my body. Terrible!

BL: At this moment, as you are thinking that and reacting, are you on the table at this point, or are you standing there just remembering? What is happening?

NL: I'm on the table, and there's a hose going up into my vagina. There's three of them down there, and they're intent, pulling something out of me.

BL: Do you feel any discomfort or pain? Are you feeling any of that?

NL: I feel some cramping in my abdomen.

BL: Describe the hose.

NL: I think it's a vacuum.

BL: Is there a sense of pulling something out?

NL: Yes, there's suction to it.

BL: Now, we can slow down this experience, no matter how fast they're going with what they're doing, so let's slow it down and look at the three guys there. First, do you have the impression that they look similar to each other?

NL: Yes, they all look the same. They look like the little grey ones, but a little bit taller. Maybe it's because I'm lying down.

BL: That's right. You have a different perspective.

NL: They're taking something from me.

BL: What comes to mind? What do you think they're taking from you?

NL: It makes me think of abortion.

BL: So, they're taking something from you now. You mentioned earlier that they assigned somebody to you to keep you calm. Is there anybody there with you right now on this table with this procedure happening?

NL: The same one is still on my right arm. She's there. I don't know why I think it's a female, but maybe because she is in my head.

BL: What does she seem to be doing?

NL: She is just doing her job, keeping me calm. There's no complication to it. She just has one simple focus, and that's for me to stay calm.

BL: Is she communicating anything else to you?

NL: She's making me feel it's okay and that everything is all right. She wants me to believe that nothing bad is going to happen to me. That's it.

BL: Is she saying these words aloud?

NL: No, they don't do that.

BL: Are you saying that she is speaking telepathically to you?

NL: Yes.

BL: Does this calm you down and help?

NL: Oh, yes, it works. You'd be out of your mind, screaming and fighting like crazy if they didn't do that to you, but I'm paralyzed, and I can't move. They try to make you believe it's the right thing and that it's okay. There's nothing okay about it!

BL: Yes, but they say things like that.

NL: They try to make you believe it's natural, but it's not. Nothing is right about it. Nobody asked me!

BL: You have all this influence coming to you suggesting it's okay, but can you see through it right at the same time?

NL: Yes. I don't believe it. I know when I'm with perpetrators. It's all so unbelievable!

BL: Take a good look at this one to your right. What does she look like?

NL: It's funny how they blur everything, but when you look hard, you get something different.

BL: Yes, that's true.

NL: I think she may not even be a Grey. She looks like a mixture of something and has that female look to her. Wow! I wonder if I know her! It's interesting, but I get the feeling she doesn't want to be there either.

BL: Do you get the sense that she is a human female or maybe some other kind of female?

NL: I think they have done something to her. I don't know what she is. She's a mix of something. It's not a good thing.

BL: What thoughts do you have about that?

NL: She is a mixture of something. Yes.

BL: So, you think she doesn't want to be there either?

NL: Yes. It seems like slavery in a controlled society where it's not good or kind.

BL: Do you have a sense that all of these beings, whatever they are, are doing this routinely without any agenda?

NL: There is an agenda. Of course, they want something.

BL: And right now concerning you, what does it seem like their agenda is?

NL: Right now, it's just physical information. It's always about gathering information.

BL: So, do you think that whatever they're doing now by taking something out of your body with an instrument is for their purpose of learning?

NL: You know what else? They're also fascinated with my breasts! [*At the time, I had breast implants.*]

BL: Are they examining you there now, too?

NL: They put something into my right breast.

BL: This is a personal thing for you. How are you reacting to them doing this to you?

NL: Well, I'm incredibly subdued. My terror was overwhelming, but now I feel like I've been shot full of drugs. They want to watch your progress all the time to see how things are progressing.

BL: Specifically, is it your breast or your reproductive organs that they are mainly focusing on?

NL: Oh, both.

BL: Do you have a sense that they're talking or communicating with each other in any way as they examine you?

NL: I can't tell because my emotions are so dead, but there may be communication going on with someone to the side. It's so shocking, so unbelievable! I don't ever remember anything like this. It's all you can do to accept it.

BL: Which, of course, is what they want you to do.

NL: Yes.

BL: With all of the events happening now, do you think these kinds of procedures have ever happened before to you? Is it familiar to you?

NL: I may remember something from when I was younger. Believe it or not, but I think my father is here, too.

BL: When you say he is here, too, is that strange for him to be here in this environment where this stuff is happening?

NL: He's somewhere nearby. I knew it happened to him, too. I knew it did, but I didn't want to believe it.

BL: No, and probably he doesn't want to believe it either. Do you think he's there also as a victim?

NL: Yes. He's completely out of it.

BL: So, you are both having a very unusual and invasive experience. Do you have a sense that he might even be in the same room?

NL: Yes, he is off to the side. I have to get out of here now!

BL: Yes, we are going to leave it now because of the time.

(End of Excerpt)

© 2020 Nadine Lalich

Reptilian

Tall White

3
EARLY MEMORIES

The 1962 Visitation

The earliest memory I have of possible ET contact happened in 1962 when I was ten years old. It came back to me again in a dream during May of 1991, one month before my trip to Sedona, Arizona, where I had my first conscious abduction. I had gone to bed that night at about 9:00 p.m., and my mother, father, and brother were still up watching television. Several hours later, I woke up and walked into the dark living room where I found the three of them still sitting on the couch. They looked strange, not moving, and slumped over with their eyes partly open or closed as if they were in a trance. In those days, when a television station stopped programming for the day, a large round symbol would be displayed on the screen, and there was sometimes a droning sound in the background. I remember thinking to myself when I looked at the screen and heard the sound coming from it that the ETs could use it to control us.

It was summertime, and the front door had been left open with the wooden screen door locked. I stared through the screen into the darkness, and I recall seeing a giant UFO hovering above the street. The craft was so big that it extended over the houses on both sides of the road. A beam was shooting down from the ship, and I knew that someone was coming to see me. In a few moments, someone was standing on the porch, so I unlocked the door and held it open for him to enter. We stepped into the small dining room where the light over the kitchen table was on, and I sat down in a chair. My family remained subdued in the living room and did not respond.

The man looked odd to me with his white skin and short, stocky frame. His eyes were slanted, and his ears were large and pointed. His mouth was large and full, and he held a small tubular instrument between his thin lips. Strangely, he also wore a blue short-sleeved tee-shirt, perhaps to make himself look more human. I knew right away that he could read my mind and that he was aware that I was suffering emotionally from past trauma in my childhood.

He stood before me, where I sat and took my wrist into his hand. Telepathically he asked me if I wanted to have my pain taken away. Although I was not afraid of him, I was still in shock by his presence, and I did not respond. He then moved my wrist to his mouth and against the apparatus he was holding there. At the same time, he touched my head with his other hand, and a great shock went through me. My head fell backward with my mouth open, and I let out a scream. It was far beyond telepathy as if he had stepped into my mind and could peer into every corner of my brain to see all of my memories. It was an invasive feeling as though two people were in my body at one time. I also knew that he, too, was now experiencing all of my suppressed emotional pain. After about a minute, the emotional intensity began to subside, as if the energy attached to the memories was slowly draining away. He held my head in that position for another minute, then withdrew his hands, and my head fell forward.

Family in Front of Television

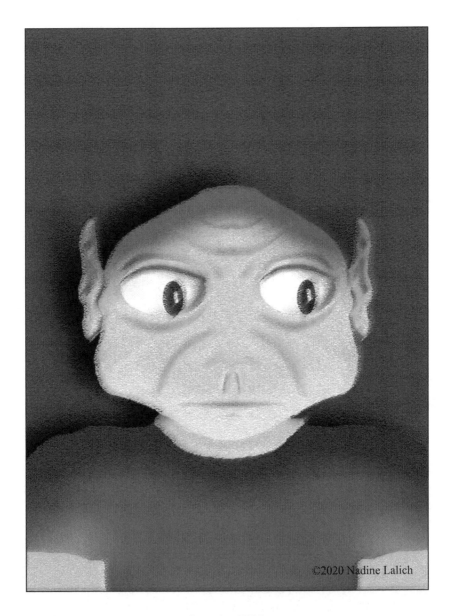

Stocky Elf

I sensed that he was pleased with what he had done, and for the first time in my life, it felt as though someone understood me intimately. The event ended with him abruptly walking out of the door and disappearing. This was one of the rare experiences when I thought an ET was solely there for my benefit.

Double Abduction in Metro Park 1968

An early memory of contact occurred in 1968 while I was in the company of another person. Initially, because the event was disturbing, I chose to dismiss it at the time as being impossible. Once I began to face my ET experiences, the incident resurfaced, and I was able to accept the memory of the low-flying, saucer-shaped craft, we had seen that summer evening in Michigan.

On that particular night, my boyfriend, Mike, and I went for a long drive into the countryside to Metro Park, which was a favorite spot of ours. While parked on the side of a dark road, we saw what appeared to be a large metallic craft flying directly overhead. It seemed to be about one hundred feet across with colored lights around the bottom. We were shocked and curious as it dropped lower directly above our vehicle, silently gliding along. Although we had shared an interest in astronomy, we had never discussed the subjects of UFOs or alien life. As it was slowly passing us, we decided to follow it. Several hours later, we awoke on the side of the road and thought nothing of it and just assumed that we had fallen asleep. We did recall seeing the craft and were excited to tell my parents what we had seen, but they did not believe us.

Aerial View of Huron Metropolitan Park

Craft Hovering Over Car

The following is a hypnotic regression conducted by Barbara Lamb on February 12, 2005, regarding the event.

BL: So today, Nadine, we are going to do a regression, and we are going back to that experience that you had in the summer of 1968 when you were sixteen years old, and you were with your boyfriend, Mike, driving on a rural road. In that experience, you saw a large ship up in the air with a round dome on the top, and you watched it until it came down near the ground. We are going to go back now to that experience and pick up all of the details that you consciously remember, as well as anything else that you were not consciously aware of at the time. We are going back to the entire experience of that summer night in 1968 when you were sixteen years old, driving along the rural road with Mike, and seeing an unusual sight. To do that, we're going into a pleasant state of deep relaxation, back to that summer of 1968 when you were driving with your boyfriend, Mike, who was a special person to you at the time. On this rural road, both of you see a large object in the sky that's coming down near the ground. It has a round dome on the top, and you decided to follow it. What else can you see?

NL: At first, it seems like green, but maybe it's white light.

BL: Where does that white light seem to be?

NL: It's coming from underneath.

BL: Does it do anything, or just stay right by this object?

NL: At first, I thought it was short, coming out of little holes underneath it, but now it seems brighter.

BL: Do you mean that it shines outward to some extent?

NL: Yes. I also see tall weeds on the side of the road. It seems like we're slowing down.

BL: Do you think you are still looking out the window?

NL: We're really excited. I know we saw it and we're starting to follow it, but we can't believe it! The light seems whiter and bigger now.

BL: Does it still seem to be overhead?

NL: It's overhead and in front of us, but it feels like we're not in the same place where we were. I feel like he is scared all of a sudden.

BL: Is Mike scared?

NL: Yes.

BL: Is he saying anything?

NL: He is saying something, but I don't know what.

BL: You are aware that he seems to be scared, but what are you feeling?

NL: It feels like we're out of the car now, standing beside it and looking at this thing.

BL: Is it still there?

NL: Yes, and it's really slow and hovering.

BL: Has the car completely stopped now?

NL: Yes, but I think the headlights are on, though. Mike is on his side of the car, and I'm on my side, and we're looking up. It stopped moving, and now we're on a different road that's a lot smaller. There is tall grass or stalks of corn along the side of the road, but nobody is around.

BL: Is the object still there?

NL: Yes, but it's not moving.

BL: Has it come any closer than it was before?

NL: It's close, maybe 50 feet. It feels like there is a focus on him. That's sad, but I don't know why.

BL: It makes you sad to think that?

NL: Yes. He is wearing a black shirt, and it's about him this time.

BL: Now that he is out of the car and looking up, is he scared?

NL: I'm just watching, and I don't feel like I'm involved, but maybe I am. I think the light is on him, that white light.

BL: Is there a light shining directly on him?

NL: Yes, and his body seems to be twisted.

BL: Take a look at that light. Is it just an area of light, or does it have more of a shape to it?

NL: It's a beam, and it has shiny particles in it, but I don't know what it does.

BL: Is this beam coming right down to him?

NL: It's on him where he is on the other side of the car. I'm not moving much over here in the dark. I'm not standing in the light.

BL: Are you able to move? Have you tried to move?

NL: I don't think I can. I'm leaning on the car. I feel bad for him because he is so terrified.

BL: How do you feel over on your side of the car?

NL: I feel dull and numb. The only thing I can feel is feeling sorry for him. I want to help him, but I can't!

BL: What makes you think you can't help him?

NL: I don't know. I'm in the dark on the other side of the car, and I'm not a part of it.

BL: Does it seem to be focused only on him?

NL: Yes, but you know what? I think there is somebody behind me in the tall grass because I hear a rustling. I don't know what that is. Actually, I think there is some activity going on around both of us suddenly. It looks like he is frozen in this position. He looks weird.

BL: Do you see anybody near him, or do you just see him in the light?

NL: Some of them are coming out in a circle around us all of a sudden. They're curious about him, but I think they know me.

BL: Are they all focused on him?

NL: Yes.

BL: Don't you feel that any of their attention is on you?

NL: No, but I feel like they know me, and I'm just waiting. I don't know what they're doing with him, but I'm waiting.

BL: Just notice what does happen now, whatever it is that you can see or be aware of in any way.

NL: I think he is just gone for a while, and I'm outside waiting. Somebody is here waiting with me.

BL: Okay, now let's slow it down here and go back to that point where they're all around, and it seems like their focus is on him. Just notice anything that happens that causes you to realize that he's gone.

NL: Somebody touched me on the shoulder and made me stop moving. I don't know what to do. I wasn't present for a minute, and now he's not there anymore, but the ship is still here.

BL: Is the beam of light there any longer?

NL: No. It's misty and grey out, but still a little lighter around me somehow.

BL: Is there is a light around you now as you are standing next to the car?

NL: Yes.

BL: Is the whole beam of light gone now?

NL: Yes.

BL: Now that he is gone, do you notice anything that's happening for you?

NL: I don't like being on the road by myself like that.

BL: Are you completely alone, or does it seem like somebody else is there?

NL: Somebody is here with me, one of them. He is shorter and smaller, behind me, and keeping me calm and patient.

BL: How does it seem like this one is doing that?

NL: I think he touched the inside of my arm or my wrist. I think it has something to do with my body endorphins relaxing or sedating me. I can feel those long fingers.

BL: What do they feel like?

NL: Rubber.

BL: Now, this is summer, so are your arms bare? Can you get the sense of that feeling?

NL: Yes, my arms are bare.

BL: How would you describe what you feel?

NL: It's a little creepy. They move so slow and deliberate. It has something to do with the inside of my right elbow, pressing it with his finger.

BL: Can you tell just by the feeling of it how many fingers there are?

NL: There are three fingers, and a thumb is behind the other side of my elbow.

BL: What did you say the texture feels like?

NL: I might be kidding myself.

BL: You might be kidding yourself about what?

NL: About being where I am. I feel the metal.

BL: Well, let us just notice anything else.

NL: I might be inside.

BL: We're talking now about the kinesthetic feeling, but you can also notice whatever you see, visually. You have been feeling the three fingers and the thumb on your elbow. Just keep on feeling and noticing visually.

NL: I might be inside. I see him ahead of me. I don't know if this is real.

BL: Just put aside any evaluating and notice what you do see.

NL: All right then, I'm inside a dark round room, and I see Mike on a table.

BL: What does the table look like?

NL: It's a metal table. I see him without a shirt on, and he is really fighting, really freaked out. Oh God! I think they're sticking something in his penis!

BL: Well, just go with what you are seeing. You see him on the table. Is he sitting on the table without a shirt on?

NL: He is lying down, wanting to move, and he is freaking out.

BL: Do you see anybody else with him, or is he just by himself?

NL: I see a few of them at the foot where his legs are. It's dark at the edges, and there are some lights over him on the metal table that looks like stainless steel.

BL: Now we're going to break this down into little increments, just moment-by-moment. You are seeing a few of them at the foot of the table. Describe what they look like.

NL: I have never seen them move like this before. Their legs and arms seem particularly skinny and dangly. It's like they're moving a little bit in slow motion, and their heads are enormous with little, teeny holes for the nose. I can barely see the mouth. I don't know why, but they seem taller than usual.

BL: They seem taller than what?

NL: They're like the others I've seen, but just a little taller for some reason.

BL: What do their eyes look like?

NL: Black.

BL: How about the shape?

NL: They are big, almond-shaped and black. They're intently focusing on him, and they seem bothered that he is so upset. They're running around. Oh, man!

BL: Notice what they seem intent on and if it makes sense to you.

NL: They're doing something to his genital area, putting something long into his penis. Yuck!

BL: Can you get any sense of what that is that they're putting in there?

NL: It looks like a glass tube. It's a thin, long glass tube with a round bulb thing at the end.

BL: Is the glass tube is empty?

NL: There is some liquid in it, a clear liquid in a thin glass tube going somewhere.

BL: How is he reacting to this?

NL: Oh, he's terrified.

BL: So it seems like he's conscious and aware?

NL: He's calming down now, but at first, he was flailing all over, trying to hold his legs together.

BL: Are they trying to hold his legs apart?

NL: Yes.

BL: Are they still doing this procedure right now?

NL: They've taken something from him and put it in a little transparent, round case.

BL: Is that something a fluid?

NL: It could be. It's white and cloudy, and it could be sperm floating in water in the round tray. It's a clear tray, and the top comes off it. I think he's tagged with something, a computer chip in his foot. They're doing that, too. Wow!

BL: At this particular time, what does it seem like they are doing with his foot?

NL: They did something to his foot, his arch, or his heel. They put something in it, and then they made the skin close up by placing a light on it.

BL: Just notice now. You can slow this down if you want to. Replay it to get more details.

NL: I can see the hair on his legs and his right foot.

BL: Where do you seem to be? Are you getting a good view?

NL: He is on the table, and I'm next to him, sitting on some kind of chair. Someone is with me and holding my elbow. That's it.

BL: Now that feeling of someone holding you on the elbow, does it feel like it did down on the ground?

NL: Yes, it's the same thing and the same being.

BL: Your right elbow?

NL: Yes, they're pressing inside. They press the wrist, too, at the inside of the wrist. He took his fingers from inside my elbow and pressed three fingers from one side of my wrist, and the thumb is underneath. There is something specific about the pressure.

BL: Do you have a sense that they know exactly where to press?

NL: Oh, yes, they know everything.

BL: And the effect of their pressing? What effect does that seem to have?

NL: You don't move. You're paralyzed, and you can barely feel your body. It numbs you. I don't think it is so much emotional as it is physiological, stopping your body's response.

BL: Does it stop your emotions, too?

NL: I'm calm, but that might be from something else. I'm mentally here with him and disturbed that he is going through this, but I don't really feel my feelings.

BL: Do you know if he has ever had experiences like this before?

NL: No. I don't know anything.

BL: Do you think that Mike has any sense that you are right there?

NL: No, I don't think he is paying any attention to me.

BL: Okay.

NL: I wonder if what they did to me gave me the endometriosis I suffered with for years. I would tell them to leave him alone! Why are you doing that? He's at Mike's right leg, and he turned around and looked at me. There is somebody in the background, one of the big white guys standing in the shadows. He's the leader. I know he was there from the beginning. You know, when you imagine yourself filled with white light, feeling surrounded by love, that scares them off sometimes. It strikes them oddly, puts them off, and makes them stand back.

BL: Maybe they're not so in touch with the white light.

NL: No, they are, but they just take the energy and use it mechanically for manipulation, not for evolution. I use it for the development of my psyche and my soul. When you have the emotional side as a human being, you understand that the power of the light affects the soul, but they can't use it that way because they don't feel that part of themselves. They're dead to it so they can't apply it in that way. No wonder they want what we have, but they can't get it that way!

BL: Okay, so we're now withdrawing slowly from that whole scene with him, you, and with the beings. We are going to bring our attention back to the car. Notice how you returned to the car that night.

NL: It's dark. The lights are off, and the car isn't running. We're sitting in the car, and it's as though we fell asleep.

BL: Oh, you're already sitting in the car?

NL: We're sitting parked in the dark. Mike's head is leaning backward, and his Adam's apple is sticking out.

BL: What is your first awareness? Do you feel completely awake, or are you still waking up?

NL: I'm awake. He's not awake so fast and just coming to. We're not talking and just driving back to my house. We told everyone we had seen a ship. My parents thought we were nuts.
      (End of Excerpt)

Several years after our relationship had ended, I learned from his sister that he had been hospitalized for psychiatric treatment after growing increasingly paranoid. Apparently, he had become obsessed with ETs, claiming that strange beings were coming into his apartment through the walls and communicating with him. Although his doctors declared it to be the onset of schizophrenia, I do wonder if there might be a connection to continuing ET encounters that he could not live with.

4

ONGOING EXPERIENCES

Death Triggers Contact

On February 23, 2000, I returned to my home town of Lincoln Park, Michigan, to prepare my parent's house for sale. My father had passed away four days earlier, and my mother, who was suffering from early dementia, was temporarily staying with her sister until I could bring her back with me to California. The following experience I had that first night in the house was particularly lucid and detailed.

The house had been emptied of most of their belongings, but I had kept a mattress in one of the bedrooms to sleep on during my stay. I recall that it was sometime after midnight when I decided to leave the house and go out into the yard. It was a cold winter night, and in the cloudless sky, the moon appeared huge. I noticed that I was not alone; a man from the neighborhood had also come out of his house.

I looked up into the sky again and was mesmerized by several UFOs I saw overhead. There was a large ship with several smaller ones flying alongside and behind the bigger craft. I called out to the man to look up, and he did but did not respond to me. I knew they were coming for me again.

UFOs in Night Sky over Richmond Street

My knees were shaky, and I felt they would buckle at any moment, so I sat down on the cold ground. I knew the ETs were coming for me again, and I thought of going to hide, but I knew it was useless. I was determined to stay out of the trance as long as possible and to remember as many details as I could. I would also try to communicate better and ask them questions. A few minutes later, several extraterrestrials appeared, and I noted that there were three different species: a small Grey, a Tall White, and a third type that I could not identify.

My next recollection was of being on a craft, standing alone. No one seemed to be paying attention to me, but I noticed a lot of activity taking place around me with different beings coming and going from the large room. I also saw several extraterrestrials actively managing and directing a group of humans who I guessed was also abductees. I knew they did not want me to remember what was happening, but I was determined to do my best.

I lost consciousness for a while, and when I regained my awareness, I was sitting at a transparent glass or acrylic table with several unusual instruments set on top. Directly across from me sat what looked like a giant praying mantis. Although this being would appear in numerous experiences in the coming years, this was the first time I recall having seen him. I have no idea how I knew it was a male, but I did, and I also sensed he was a scientist who conducted the training.

One of the instruments set before me was a glass or acrylic box, approximately four by five inches in size, that would scan my body when the lid was lifted by shooting out a beam of light that could calculate physical information. Also on the table were about a dozen transparent glass cylinders, each filled with varying amounts of clear liquid. Etched into each tube were strange symbols, and I had the impression that the device used sound and vibration technology to program a human's mind or body. All they wanted me to do was sit and listen to the sounds it emitted.

Later they placed another transparent box in front of me about twelve inches long, five inches wide and an inch and a half thick. The box glowed from within with beautiful blue light. Compelled to lift the lid, I saw that it contained many thin, transparent sheets that I was supposed to turn like pages in a book. Each flat sheet had numerous odd cut-out shapes with an iridescent film stretched across each opening. Telepathically, the praying mantis, or Insectoid as some refer to that species, instructed me to turn each page slowly. I would then concentrate my gaze for a minute or so upon each shape until I had viewed everything on the page. Then I would flip to the next one and begin again. I believe the symbols and the membrane stretched across each one contained information much as our computer chips do. Perhaps by focusing on them and the light they emitted, data was being sent to my retinas, and then converted to neural signals in my brain. Strange as it may sound, I think they were programming my mind with information that might be retrieved or activated at a later date.

I spent a good deal of time researching the symbols of ancient texts trying to find similarities with the wavy, pointed alien symbols I have seen. The closest resemblance I could find was the ancient Phoenician alphabet. An article from the Ancient History Encyclopedia online describes the language as follows:

> Phoenician is a Canaanite language closely related to Hebrew. Very little is known about the Canaanite language, except what can be gathered from the El-Amarna letters written by Canaanite kings to Pharaohs Amenophis III (1402 - 1364 BCE) and Akhenaton (1364

- 1347 BCE). It appears that the Phoenician language, culture, and writing were strongly influenced by Egypt (which controlled Phoenicia for a long time). ... Before circa 1000 BCE Phoenician was written using cuneiform symbols that were common across Mesopotamia. The first signs of the Phoenician alphabet found at Byblos are clearly derived from Egyptian hieroglyphics, and not from cuneiform. The 22 Phoenician letters are simplifications of Egyptian hieroglyphic symbols, which took on a standardized form at the end of the 12th century BCE[4].

I was curious and not at all afraid of the Insectoid being sitting across from me. In a rare two-way telepathic conversation, my anger came across in my thoughts when I looked at the being thinking, "You are not God! You may all think that you are, but you are not!"

He responded telepathically, telling me that my concept of God was not accurate, and I should expand my thinking. He went on to say that God is not a permanent entity, and we are all a part of that force, like focal points of the energy that continues to create and expand through infinitely. As we develop, so does God. He also seemed surprised at how long I was staying awake during this experience. When I asked him why he thought that was happening, he responded that it was due to my emotional state. They believe that emotions can affect the psyche in many ways, and it was the intense emotions from my father's death that activated their attention and triggered the abduction and examination.

---

[4] Thamis, "The Phoenician Alphabet & Language," Ancient History Encyclopedia, (2012) Accessed October 16 2019, https://www.ancient.eu/article/17/the-phoenician-alphabet--language.

Audio Tube Testing with Insectoid Being

Absorbing Information from Computer Light Box

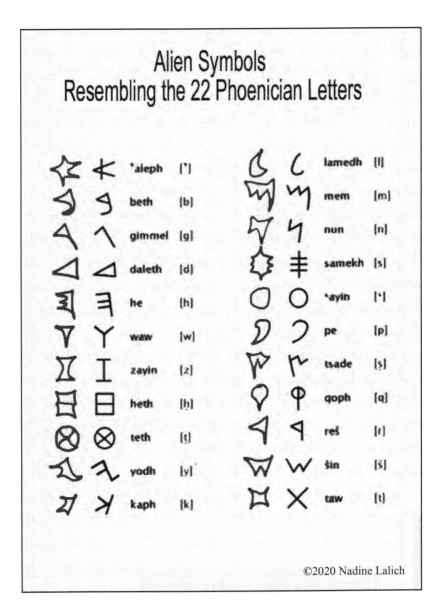

Alien Symbols

I became aware that I was not wearing any clothing, and that I was sitting in a chair with an opening in the back. While I had been sitting at the table, someone was behind me, probing my back through the chair opening. I wondered if he was helping my body or hurting me by some experiment. I also thought he did something to my head and the left side of my neck and ear. My low back began to hurt, and I tried to pull away, but I could not because something was keeping me in the chair.

There was a Tall White also in the room standing at a distance working at an instrument panel along the wall. He glanced my way, and I felt distinct agitation from him. A Grey female then approached from my left and leaned over me, placing several identical items onto the table. The object directly in front of me was a rounded transparent tray with a curved lid about two inches in diameter. Through the top, I saw what appeared to be a centipede, and I worried that they wanted me to eat it. Another female who looked somewhat human appeared to the right side of the table, but I realized they were probably altering my perception. In my mind, I asked her if they found humans repulsive, and she responded affirmatively.

I lost consciousness then, and when I became aware again, I saw that bug trays were gone. I was still sitting at the table, but the females were gone, and someone else was watching me from across the table. The symbol box was in front of me, and I knew they wanted me to look at the symbol sheets again, but I hesitated and kept asking him questions in my mind.

The following is a transcript from a hypnotic regression conducted on January 27, 2005, by Barbara Lamb regarding the incident.

BL: Today we are going to do a regression back to the night of February 23, 2000, when you were closing up your father's house after he had died recently. We are going back to February 23, 2000, at about 3:30 a.m. when you suddenly came to and found yourself sitting upright on a mattress on the bedroom floor where you had been sleeping. In this experience, you are awake and aware that you are sitting up, experiencing heart palpitations and sweating. You were so emotionally affected by the event that you wrote in your journal for over an hour. This is the experience that we are going to go back to now. Tell me, what is the first thing that you're sensing as you're sitting on the mattress in the bedroom?

NL: I feel like someone's outside the window, at the side of the house.

BL: Are you on the first floor of this house?

NL: Yes.

BL: You have the sense that you actually see this, or are you just sensing that someone is outside the window?

NL: I sense that someone is outside the window.

BL: Do you have any particular feelings about that?

NL: It's like what happened in Santa Fe. I would feel them outside the bedroom window where I was sleeping.

BL: As much as possible, be there completely now. Be on the floor lying on the mattress when you have this awareness. Notice the position that you are in.

NL: I'm not lying down.

BL: What position are you in?

NL: I'm sitting straight.

BL: Are you leaning against anything? Are your eyes open at this point?

NL: My legs are folded underneath me, and I'm sitting cross-legged.

BL: Does that seem reasonable to you, that you would be sitting up like that?

NL: Not really. My back feels straight and rigid.

BL: Does that take some effort? What else are you aware of now besides your position?

NL: I feel as if I'm being watched.

BL: From where? From which direction?

NL: Someone is behind me watching.

BL: And how are you reacting to that?

NL: Irritated. I feel damp, cold, and irritated.

BL: And the dampness and the cold feeling, is that something that you had before you went to bed on that mattress?

NL: No. I'm feeling something like metal now, pressed against my back like a straight-backed chair with ribs across it.

BL: So, is it pressing into your back?

NL: I'm pressed and flattened against it, almost as if I'm tied to it.

BL: Emotionally, how are you doing with this?

NL: I'm irritated and angry. It's like the first time, but I'm just fed up and tired of it.

BL: Is this reminding you of something that has happened earlier? Is there something familiar about this?

NL: I'm just tired of it happening and tired of being pushed around.

BL: Has this happened before?

NL: I know them. I know the guy across the table.

BL: Have you changed your location at all? Are you talking about a guy across the table? What are you aware of now? You said you were sitting up on the mattress, and you have felt this thing press against you.

NL: I'm not on the mattress. I'm sitting at a table that feels like the tabletop is glass, but underneath is stainless steel.

BL: And how about the temperature of that?

NL: It's warmer now.

BL: So, it seems like you're in a different location and not on the mattress in the bedroom anymore, right?

NL: Yes, and the tabletop is glass with a three-inch lip around the side. It's thick and smooth glass.

BL: Is it comfortable to sit on?

NL: I'm not sitting on the table. That's in front of me. I'm sitting on some kind of chair. My back is pressed against something, and it's cold. In front, its smooth glass and I can see the table legs underneath. They're wider at the top and get smaller at the bottom.

BL: How far in front of you, are you focusing?

NL: It's right in front of me. I can't move, and my legs are bent at the knee.

BL: Are your legs touching a floor?

NL: I can't feel my legs very well, but I could be sitting.

BL: Are you feeling any discomfort in any way?

NL: My lower back aches. I want to touch the table because it looks so soft and so smooth.

BL: Yes, and when the glass comes to an end, it's like round at the end. It's perfect and smooth. Is there any color to that?

NL: No, everything is pale and grey, clear glass, or metal. This table is almost pretty.

BL: What is the lighting like?

NL: The lighting seems to come from everywhere, but I can't tell where it comes from. Everything is lit up, but not brightly. Then there's a separate light in the center of the table, underneath the vials and tubes. There's a light shining up from under the table, too. The cylinders have liquid in them, and each one is at a different level. Wow! It makes me think of a musical instrument.

BL: Are these lined up next to each other?

NL: They're in the center of the table, a bunch of them placed in a circle. Some are tall and others short, but they're all filled with different amounts of clear liquid. It seems like it has something to do with hearing or sound. The guy across from me is the same one who was across the room from me the first time in Sedona, the one with the funny head that looked like an insect. The pasty-white guy is in the background that I don't like, and he's annoyed by me.

BL: The one in the background looks familiar to you?

NL: He looks familiar to me, and we don't like each other much.

BL: Let's pause for a minute and take a good look at him. What does he look like?

NL: I wonder why it's so hard to look at him. I feel like I can't move my head up to look at him even though he's right in front of me, looking at me so intently. He knows that I'm determined to remember, and I'm going to be present. That's all there is to it!

BL: Good.

NL: There's a female here to the right of me and someone else behind. The guy across from me wants me to do something, and I don't know why it seems to me it has something to do with my hearing. I still can't look at the one across the room, but I know I've looked at him before when he was a long way across a room.

BL: Okay, but he is closer now, right?

NL: He's much closer.

BL: Now, are you afraid to look at his eyes?

NL: He's not like the other ones, and it seems like his eyes are more on the side of his head, with little sections to the eyes.

BL: Facets, sort of?

NL: Yes. Facets and little bumps in the eye, and his head comes out more.

BL: His face?

NL: Yes, a different shape that's broader at the top and then goes in and out again at the chin. He has a mouth and eyes like a fly, not black. They're reddish or brownish-black with separations, like little cells in the eye.

BL: His skin?

NL: It's white like chalk.

BL: From where you are sitting, does this one in the background seem to be about your height, or does he seem to be shorter or taller?

NL: He's bigger and much taller than I am. I think he's the same one that watched me the first time. He has that same look.

BL: Do you think he is the same type of being, or do you think he is the same individual? Can you determine that?

NL: I think he's the same being, the same one from Sedona, when I walked into the craft the first time. He was standing on the other side of the room and seemed so emotionally cold. He's cold now, but he's more curious and irritated because I'm fighting.

BL: What is it about him that makes you feel sure that he is irritated? Is he showing it with facial expressions?

NL: No, I can feel it because he's trying to do something in my head, and I'm resisting him, fighting him a lot now. I'm not afraid like I was, so I'm annoying to them. I kept thinking that when I got older, this was not going to be happening anymore.

BL: What is it about your age that you think would mean this would not be happening now?

NL: It's because I'm in menopause.

BL: Are you surprised because being in menopause does not seem to make a difference to them? Does your reproductive functioning have anything to do with how you feel about this?

NL: I think it happens in stages. For ten years, they treat you one way. In the next ten years, you're studied another way. Every ten years, there's something different.

BL: Are you just talking about your regular cycles as a woman?

NL: Yes, that's how they break it up.

BL: Do you have a sense that they have studied you in these ten-year cycles, and that has been going on for quite a while, longer than you thought?

NL: I think it's a part of my life, and it has been a part of my father's life. They're more curious about me now, though, because I'm resisting, and I'm irritated. I'm not so scared anymore, and I hate it all. It's not fair! Someone else is here now, to my left, a female that I have seen before. She seems like she is in her early twenties, and they want to see how I act when I see her. She is drawn to me and standing by me now.

BL: What kind of feeling do you get emanating from her?

NL: I feel sorry for her. She seems lost somehow and not free.

BL: How about describing her?

NL: She is tall with thin, wispy blond hair on her head like baby hair, cut short. Something is not right with her skin, or it's so transparent you can see through it to the veins. Her eyes are pretty and different with big eyelids and lashes. I also remember having had profound memories of seeing her when she was a child.

BL: Does she have lashes?

NL: Yes, and she has lips. She's pretty.

BL: Does she seem to be registering anything now you are looking at her? Is she looking at you?

NL: She was looking at me, apparently fascinated by me more than I realized. I think she wants to touch my shoulder.

BL: Would you say that she's a human being, or is she somewhat different from that?

NL: Something is not right with her. She's detached and sad.

BL: Does she touch you?

NL: She is standing next to me, touching my shoulder and the edge of the chair. I know she has just been out on a few occasions, but she never stays long, and I don't know where she goes.

BL: The one you were just looking at with the blonde hair, did she seem tall?

NL: Tall like me, but not extremely tall.

BL: Tall like a regular human woman?

NL: Five feet seven or eight.

BL: Have you been aware all through this?

NL: Well, they do something here to keep you emotionally calm when they do this.

BL: So they actually press your wrist?

NL: Yes. They press it or make energy go into the area. I remember the first time that they did that, she never left my wrist. She was there the whole time.

BL: Okay. What else is happening?

NL: I want to touch this thing on the table, to look at these symbols in the clear case. It closes, and then when you open it up, there is a bunch of them in there, not just one. All the transparent sheets are hooked together at the bottom, like the spine of a book. Each symbol has a meaning. At first, it looks as though you could poke your finger through the shapes, but you can't because the design is covered with a thin, iridescent film of some kind. I'm supposed to flip through the sheets to learn from them, and I'm tempted to touch them.

BL: Do they want you to?

Adult Female Hybrid

Child Female Hybrid

NL: Yes, absolutely. They want me to remember these, but I don't understand the meaning of the symbols. They're supposed to tell me something later. If I remember them now, then I will remember them later when I see them. They're all pointy, and each one contains information. Altogether, it has to be memorized.

BL: And they're watching you as you're handling this?

NL: Yes, they're watching in front of me. The thing that I thought looked like a centipede in the clear, round tray is metal. It's in the glass tray with a lubricant. The top lid is a magnifier, so it makes the thing inside look bigger. I just realized that I'm not alone at the table. There are others like me.

BL: Do you mean more humans?

NL: Yes, and I think the table is longer than I thought, and I have just been focusing on one end of it. There are other humans here, but they don't have the symbol box. They're doing something with everyone. I thought that they wanted me to eat that thing, but now I don't think so.

BL: What thing?

Implant in Magnifying Container

NL: The thing in the tray that I thought looked like a centipede. Actually, I can see that it's a lot smaller with many little legs on it like a little comb. They don't want me to eat it because it has something to do with my ear. They kept it in this liquid to keep it clean. They distract you by having you look at something while they're doing something else to you.

BL: Are you in front of it? What's on the table?

NL: The box of symbol sheets is on the table.

BL: So, you do have two things to concentrate on. There are the sheets with symbols and the tray of liquid with the object in. I that right?

NL: They're doing something with the little metal object. All I have to do with is look at the symbols sheets. I know they're trying to put the information into my head that they can get out later. I think the film in the center of the symbols has something to do with the information. There's more meaning to the symbols than just their shape. Each one also contains information within it, like a computer chip. The film is pearly and reflects pale colors like a rainbow.

BL: Would you say that it's pretty?

NL: Yes, like sheets of geometrical shapes that you use for drawing. I'm wondering how these glass tubes have anything to do with my ears or measuring my hearing. I think someone else is watching me.

There are three other people here at the table, too.

BL: Are you the only one looking at the symbol sheets?

NL: Oh, yes. I'm looking at the symbol sheets, and they watch me when I do it.

BL: By "they," do you mean the other types who are not like you?

NL: Yes, they're watching, me but there are other humans at the table, too, who aren't a part of this, and they seem like they're asleep. Maybe they test one person at a time.

BL: How many beings would you say are watching you as you are looking at the symbol sheets?

NL: There's the one in front, and across the table, the girl to the right who's supposed to keep me calm, and someone is behind me doing something to my back, but he's not paying attention to that thing on the table. He doesn't care, and he's just manually doing something. There are three or four of them also standing behind me, and they're exchanging thoughts as they look at me and watch in my head. They see in my head, and then they communicate, but I can't tell what they're thinking, and I can't hear them.

BL: You can't tell what they're thinking?

NL: No.

BL: How do you know that they're communicating with each other?

NL: I can feel it in my head. He wants them to notice me. Yes, I think he likes me, after all.

BL: Does it seem like he's in favor of the way that you're responding to these sheets of information?

NL: I think that when you do the right thing, it surprises them, and they don't like it, but they respect you.

BL: Are they in a trance or whatever?

NL: Oh, yes.

BL: And they know that you are more aware, right?

NL: They communicated about it. They think some kinds of emotions make us stay awake more, and they like to watch that happening because they believe it affects our perception. They want to know what feeling does to perception because they're not like that.

BL: Okay. Do you have the feeling that you're being more aware of what you're doing than the other ones at the table?

NL: Oh, yes.

BL: Do you think that your emotion does something to your perceptions?

NL: It can bring you closer to something and give you extra insight into what you see. It gives you a foundation to hold on to if you are scared, but if you're too afraid, it shuts everything out. If you're passionate, in a positive way, it wakes you up, and you see more.

BL: So, some emotion is helpful.

NL: It's energy. I guess its strength.

BL: Do you think that it's your emotional energy that makes you remember these experiences?

NL: I want to know what they're doing. I don't trust them, and I never have. I don't like the way they do it, and I want to know what's going on. Finding out and understanding is a power that gives you strength.

BL: You mean the things they have you doing here?

NL: No. It's not just this. This is nothing. This is easy.

BL: It's easy compared to what?

NL: Some of the stuff is bad, and it's just not right. If I have to be bothered with this stuff, I'm going to watch and see everything and learn. I don't know, but I'm not afraid anymore.

BL: Good.

NL: Sometimes when you're angry, it's a good thing.

BL: It's strengthening.

NL: Yes, it can be so long as it's not irrational.

BL: So right now in this situation, by the table and these other beings and everything, you're not feeling scared?

NL: No.

BL: Good. You're really paying attention. Is that right?

NL: I do now.

BL: Do you feel mentally clear in this setting, sitting by the table and the information sheets and noticing what you notice?

NL: Yes, but I'm still fuzzy. It's like a cloud pulled over you, and you have to strain and push to see. You have to work hard for clarity.

BL: Sure. You're doing some of that, aren't you?

NL: I see more all the time.

BL: So at this table now, you're straining to see what's happening?

NL: Because I do work so hard to see, they think I'm interesting, maybe valuable. Some push through, and some don't.

BL: Do you feel that these sheets of information are making sense?

NL: No. I think that if you look at it, you remember it even though you don't realize it. I think you're getting the information stored in the brain and, later on, when you see something, you'll know it. I'm not fighting it. I'm cooperating because I'll use it, too.

BL: I suppose there's a chance that maybe they want you to do something in the future. What sense do you have about that?

NL: I was standing in a dark room, and there was this picture screen in the room.

BL: In their territory, would you say?

NL: Oh, yes. It was dark in that room, and they were showing bad things, and they wanted me to look at them. Things were blowing up, you know? Something is going to hit the earth.

BL: Is that the sort of thing they were showing you that something's going to be hitting the earth?

NL: It's going to get here. Maybe something is going to hit.

BL: Is it hard to look at it?

NL: Yes, like looking at war, but it's not war. It's just things falling apart and collapsing, blowing up with lots of smoke when something hits us that came from somewhere else.

BL: Are you frightened?

NL: Not really. I'm so tired of being afraid of everything in life. I know everything is going to be okay. I trust in the order of things, and I trust in God that it's all part of a process, and I'm only here for a while anyway. There's that question, though, about how should we prepare? I have food and shelter, sleeping bags, and water ready, and I'm waiting. I'm getting ready.

BL: Do you think that maybe some of that could be stimulated by the scene that you are watching on the wall, as well as what we hear right here?

NL: I don't know. I think about survival a lot about being prepared so I can take care of myself. I want to take medical classes and CPR to be ready. I want to be self-contained, mobile, and prepared.

BL: Let us go back to sitting at the table with the guy in front looking at you and those behind, talking about you. See if you can tune in more to what the ones behind you seem to be saying to the one in front of you and vice-versa.

NL: I think the one across from me is trying to convince them of something about me. It's as if those beings behind me are mentally connected, almost as if they are operating as one entity.

BL: Are they all the same species? Can you tell?

NL: I can't tell because they're behind me.

BL: And you can't turn around?

NL: I tried to turn my head, but you can't move in this seat. I don't know who they are, but he's showing me to them, and they're skeptical. It's almost as though he's proud of me, although there's no emotion as if I'm an experiment.

BL: How old were you when you met him?

NL: Two. I get two.

BL: Okay.

NL: They put something in my body for recording. I want to know how they find me.

BL: Okay.

NL: He told me I had five. There's five. One has these little things on the bottom, small dots, and fibers that touch you, but it's tiny. There's also one that looks like a centipede and another that's black. There's a long, thin implant in my nose! What else is there? There's a rounded, silver implant. This makes me think of all the body stuff, and it's a turn-off!

BL: Do you mean things that have been done to your body?

NL: Yes, and it's disgusting. I don't want to think about it, but they can monitor everything from your temperature to everything else going on in your body. It's amazing!

BL: Do you think they're doing that right now?

NL: I think there's a whole record of everything. They can see changes when your emotions get intense, and it gets their attention. It alerts them that something's happening that's triggering intense feelings, maybe because intense emotion affects blood pressure. Who knows what else it does in the brain! There may be something at the base of my skull and the bottom of my tailbone.

BL: What is it about that at the base of the neck?

NL: I think that when they examine you and put that instrument into your colon, it serves as an x-ray device and has nothing to do with a person's sexuality. It's like an MRI but from the inside.

BL: They certainly seem to have great interest.

NL: I wonder about the chakras and if they have some way of recording disruptions of the energy meridians in the body. Maybe that's why they don't get sick because they know how to change their energy. I have so many questions.

BL: What's going to happen to the earth, and when is it going to happen?

NL: I'm seeing that something cataclysmic is going to happen that comes here from the outer atmosphere. Is it an asteroid? I think a huge asteroid or another race of beings that are on their way here that will knock the earth off its axis. It feels like tsunamis are part of it when something comes here from somewhere else and hits us. I feel like I'm supposed to help others to prepare.

BL: Are the extraterrestrials telling you to do that?

NL: They want me to be ready in a way that serves them. They don't necessarily care if it helps me. They're not concerned about me. It's about the planet. They don't care about me except that I'm a curiosity and something that will serve them. The others are still asleep and slumped over.

BL: You said there were other humans there now. Is that right?

NL: Yes.

BL: But, you're aware, and you're not slumped over like the others are.

NL: Yes. I don't know what happened here, but it seems like somebody was trying to prove something.

BL: The being in front of you?

NL: Yes. They're all surprised at how awake I am.

BL: We're going to have to conclude this, but see if there's anything else you want to see now.

NL: Okay. The one across from me is intrigued by my fighting spirit and thinks I'm more assertive and direct than most of the humans they work with.

BL: Could you imagine him smiling or showing any facial gestures?

NL: No. They're not like that. They're not colorful, and they don't have that range of possibilities at all. It's just missing. If you don't have emotions, you lose a whole other dimension, so they're missing a lot, and they can't seem to manufacture it.

BL: Do you think there's a possibility that in studying you and your reactions and the chemicals that flow through your body that they're collecting a lot of data?

NL: Oh, yes. I think the ETs identify with the physical aspect and how the organism works, but they can't determine how our feelings color perceptions and affect the physiology. They can't grasp how and why things stir us emotionally, so much that it makes our heart rate jump. In their reality, storage is based on what they've actually experienced, not what they're imagining. We exist in an almost multi-dimensional state, and they can only grasp one of our dimensions. Of course, they're in another dimensional state where we can't understand all of their aspects. It's like there's a piece of us that's similar in the manifested form where we can meet, but each of us exists partly in another realm where we can't meet.

BL: Did you explain that to them?

NL: Yes. I try so hard to conceptualize the emotional condition and make it more tangible, something you can touch and measure more. I think they like that.

BL: So, there was a real response there.

NL: Oh, yes! It made me feel good that I made a point.

BL: So, sometimes, and in that instance, there's real two-way communication, isn't there?

NL: Oh, there was on this occasion.
                    (End of Excerpt)

Floating Hologram Displaying Earth Disaster

The Great Arrival

On February 1, 2003, I had just fallen asleep when a loud clicking sound woke me up. I sensed that someone was in the room, but I was unable to stay awake and fell back into a deep sleep. Several hours later, I awoke again in my bed, feeling that an ET contact had just taken place. My memory of the event was quite vivid and contained many details about one or more alien races coming to Earth.

I was in a dark room, possibly on a craft, with several other people seated and watching a scene being projected within a hologram that hovered in mid-air. The pictures showed a large capsule descending from a dark sky toward the earth in an area that looked to be outside of Las Vegas, Nevada. When the capsule hit the ground, it began to spin while extending long metal arms outward that dug into the earth. The perspective then shifted within the hologram, and we saw a cut-away section showing the device digging into the ground. When it was fully underground, it rearranged itself into an enormous disk and began to spin within the cavern it had created.

Several Tall White entities in the room indicated telepathically that the technology could be used to control large numbers of people within an entire city. Their ability to control us is more than just through implants or mind scan practices. This underground technology is the most powerful method they have for mind control. They said there would be a mass migration to Earth by several off-planet species in the not too distant future, around 2027, and they will allegedly use the device to control the humans here. They also indicated that their occupation would begin in the larger urban cities and later, over time, in smaller rural communities across the globe.

Underground Alien Mind Control Device

Once the devices are buried, the rotation will accelerate and create an electromagnetic or another type of energy force that will be capable of disrupting the brain functioning of hundreds of thousands of people simultaneously, bringing about a semi-conscious, hypnotic state. These devices would allow them to monitor and manipulate people, invade their homes, and conduct massive numbers of abductions if they chose to do so. The apparatus also allows for a coordinated effort between other extraterrestrial ships in the outer reaches of Earth's atmosphere. It was a chilling thought that I did not know whether or not to believe.

One of the Tall Whites was communicating with me telepathically, suggesting that I will be assisting them in some way during their great arrival. He also said that the little wars we have on our planet are nothing, and we have no idea what a big war is. It was out of context, but he added a comment saying that it was the extraterrestrials that gave the microwave to humans.

The Tall White left the area, and I saw that most of the humans in the room were still in a trance-like state. For some reason, I was becoming more awake and aware. I realized then that we were in a huge hangar with windows along one side. I could not see any military or ETs in the room with us, so I went and looked out of the window. Outside of the building were several small runways, and in the distance, it looked like an open desert. Several small crafts were descending from a larger ship that was hovering in the air over the airfield, none of which seemed like humans created them. They were landing on the airstrip along with several familiar style human aircraft. In the far distance, I also saw a human-looking craft with both humans and extraterrestrials going on board.

I lost consciousness for a while, and when I became aware again, I was in a different room with a Tall White present who seemed to be curious about me. For some reason, it occurred to me that, like the Reptilians, the Tall Whites may know how to make themselves look more human by altering our perception. They can also materialize suddenly, and may even be present before we can see them. This particular ET was communicating in my mind, telling me that they travel through space using a method called *dimensional revolution,* which allows them to stop time. He said they do use physical crafts for a portion of their travel, then switch to dimensional travel for the remainder. With all the negative connotations presented, this experience was particularly disturbing.

Contact in Dreamland

This morning I awoke in bed as usual, but my mind was immediately flooded with a powerful dream that I had the night before on December 20, 2003. In the dream, I went outside during the middle of the night and saw many UFOs hovering in the sky. The ships were alternately appearing and then disappearing. I noted one craft, in particular, that was projecting a massive light beam down to the earth and dropping large rectangular baskets from the air that were attached to transparent parachutes. People were gathering in the street and watching the objects fall from the sky. Some others appeared terrified and were running about seeming to look for a place to hide. Some were running to hide. I went back inside the house, thinking that I needed to pack some personal items and also go to protect myself, but I had difficulty remaining lucid and alert enough to gather my belongings. Suddenly, a human-looking woman appeared in the room. I did not know her or trust her. I sensed that the being was a male who was projecting himself as a woman to manipulate me more easily. This was a confusing and uncomfortable experience that I believe was a dream or astral experience and not something that occurred in the third dimension.

Abductee Detainment Room

This experience gave me the strong impression that it was a physical event taking place. I awoke in the middle of the night on May 1, 2004, overwhelmed with the familiar feeling that they were coming again. I lost consciousness, and when I became aware again, I was in a room with many bunks or containers where people could lay down. I believed I was on a craft, and I tried to hide because I knew they would be coming soon. A male ET, strangely dressed in a dark red uniform, found me immediately. I had never seen such a strange suit before, and I wondered if it was a projection intended to disguise something else. He communicated telepathically, telling me that I was one of a group of people they had been working with for several years. A significant event would be happening in the future, and we would be called upon to act as liaisons between the aliens and humans. He also told me that my psychic powers would be accelerating over time. Although we were directly interacting, I was not able to look at his face and, therefore, I could not tell what species he was. I did get the impression that he was five or six feet tall. I also felt there were other beings in the room, but I could not see them. They sat me next to another human male about 60 years old whom I could clearly hear speaking out loud. He was upset and complaining about what was happening to him.

Sometime during this experience, I recall them showing me a hologram depicting a dozen or more large ships of different sizes traveling in the sky at night. At the same time, they impressed upon me that a variety of alien species would be coming to the earth.

I awoke in my bed, and it was still the middle of the night. After turning on the light, I found a lot of blood on my sheets and pillowcase, which appeared to be coming from my nose.

Blue Moon Abduction

It had been a full, blue moon the night of July 31, 2004. When I awoke the next day in my bedroom, I had a clear and conscious memory of this abduction experience.

I was living in Irvine, California at the time and working at a law firm in Costa Mesa. I was feeling a bit low that evening, so I decided to go to a live comedy show, and my cousin, Reggie, agreed to meet me there. I do not recall much about the show itself, but I do remember that we laughed hysterically for the two hours that we were there. Afterward, we went our separate ways, and I was driving home when I realized that I had not taken the right exit off the 405 freeway. I lost consciousness, and my next memory was of standing outside of my car along the freeway service drive. Another woman was standing beside me, whom I did not know. I remember that we were amazed when we saw that we each had similar marks that looked like red scrapes running down the front of our shoulders and arms. I lost consciousness then.

When I came to again, I was in a large, crowded room where there were different species of aliens and humans. I felt incredibly lucid and, eventually, I was forced to undergo another physical examination. At that point in my life, I was still terrified by these experiences, so I called out to God to help me. Although I have rarely been able to discern emotions in the demeanor of ETs, in this instance, I sensed amusement from them when I asked God for help.

I had been seated at a table with several ETs present. Their irreverent manner stirred a lot of anger in me, and I forgot my fear for a moment. I wanted to defend humanity, and I struggled in my mind to think of a way to do that. I tried to convey that although humans may have less brain or technological development compared to their species, we do have a dimension that they appear to be entirely without. I was speaking of the emotional aspect of humans, and the fact that they would like us to believe emotions are strictly a detriment.

My anger was intense, and I continued to mentally defend my case, telling them that emotions are an essential part of who we are as humans and far more complex and meaningful than what may appear on the surface. There have been several experiences when tried to explain emotions to ETs. In this instance, as I was struggling to think of the word "hologram," a three-foot-square hologram appeared hovering over the table. It looked like glass and moved sideways where you could see that it was a cube, but there were no pictures inside. After a few seconds, it disappeared.

During this discourse, I pointed out that their lack of emotional development suggests they are less evolved in some ways than humans. Humanity still struggles to manage negative emotions; however, our positive emotions can also motivate us in significant ways. The love and empathy that we are capable of experiencing for other living beings can inspire us to great acts of courage and service. These feelings also allow us to bond and support one another. Our emotions can inspire us to expand our spiritual nature, drive

Location of Abduction on July 31, 2004

us to higher achievement, and inspire us to create beautiful works of art. There was no direct response to my ranting, but I did feel they were intrigued by my perspective.

I had always perceived extraterrestrials as being more advanced in every way than humanity, but my opinion shifted considerably after this experience. Could it be that some races might covet aspects of our emotional nature? Their curiosity is certainly obsessive, as evidenced by their preoccupation with staging dramatic scenes to evoke our emotions. Although it is unclear how they accomplish it, many abductees report having experienced these strange manipulated scenarios during an alien abduction. If some races are genuinely incapable of experiencing emotions, their fascination would be understandable. Life surely would be far less exciting without emotions.

My next memory is of sitting at a large rectangular table with a dozen or so extraterrestrials of several different species. They were communicating with me telepathically about my thought processes and humans in general. They made me think about my brother and indicated they were interested in the close relationship we had, and the fact that we came from the same parents. My consciousness faded out then.

When my awareness returned, I was still sitting at the table. Directly across from me was a Tall White who appeared to be in charge of the group. Telepathically, he asked me if they (ETs) had ever impregnated me. I told him that I had been pregnant a couple of times. He was holding what looked like an electronic tablet that he was using to make a record. His next thought directed toward me was so clear that it seemed he was actually speaking out loud. "Then we did," he said.

In the next instant, they showed me two babies sitting on a flat cushion in another room with an observation window. I do not know if this was an actual physical room or if he was creating the picture in my mind. One of the babies was staring blankly at me, yet seemed to recognize me. I kept thinking they were doing this to get my emotional reaction. They were also trying to make a comparison between my brother's development, my babies, and me, all having come from the same genetic line.

They also told me that they were conducting abductions on that date because they wanted to see the effect of the blue moon on the human body. Interestingly, studies have shown the potential for how certain phases of the moon might affect biological rhythms and seasonal patterns of behavior and physiology in nature; animals, plants, even bacteria. An abstract posted by the National Institute of Health appeared in the US National Library of Medicine and stated in part as follows:

> ....The lunar cycle has an impact on human reproduction, in particular fertility, menstruation, and birth rate. Melatonin levels appear to correlate with the menstrual cycle. Admittance to hospitals and emergency units because of various causes (cardiovascular and acute coronary events, variceal hemorrhage, diarrhea, urinary retention) correlated with moon phases. ....[5]

Their reference to the blue moon made me wonder if that stage of the lunar cycle might be an active time of abduction for other experiencers.

---

[5] Zimecki, M., "The lunar cycle: effects on human and animal behavior and physiology," National Center for Biotechnology Information, (2006) Accessed October 8, 2019, https://www.ncbi.nlm.nih.gov/pubmed/16407788.

©2020 Nadine Lalich

Hybrid Babies through Window

They suggested another reason for my abduction on that particular evening. They were extremely curious about my desire to laugh that night, and they wanted to see what physical effects the intense laughing might have had upon my body. Interestingly, some studies have shown that laughter can reduce the stress hormones cortisol and epinephrine while causing the brain to release endorphins. Laughter may also boost the number of antibody-producing cells and enhance the effectiveness of T-cells. According to the Mayo Clinic:

> Laughter may improve your immune system. It can relieve pain…causing the body to produce its own natural painkillers. It can improve your mood…lessen your depression and anxiety and may make you feel happier.[6]

Perhaps through an implant in my body, the ETs were alerted to a shift in my body chemistry, which precipitated that night's abduction.

During this experience, I also remember seeing the unusual looking female again who had blue eyes and short, light-colored, fuzzy hair. She looked directly at me with what seemed like curiosity. I found her to be quite lovely, but from an emotional standpoint, I was deeply stirred. I felt a strange, motherly attachment to her, so I paid more attention this time. She appeared to be in her early twenties and was wearing an unattractive dress. I wondered if she could help us, or if she would even want to. I kept thinking that she was my daughter, taken from me when I was thirty or thirty-one!

---

[6] Mayo Clinic Staff, "Stress Relief from Laughter? It's no Joke," Mayo Clinic (April 5, 2019) Accessed October 5, 2019, https://www.mayoclinic.org/healthy-lifestyle/stress-management/in-depth/stress-relief/art-20044456.

I awoke from this experience in the early morning hours and immediately began writing in the journal I kept at my bedside. I wrote for fifty consecutive minutes, shocked by the amount of information I could recall and how vivid it was. During the experience, I was also surprised at how completely awake I felt. While it was taking place, I kept thinking, "I'm here! I'm really here, and I'm awake. This is really happening!" I had the overwhelming sense that it was a physical abduction, so real it was as if I had just walked from an actual physical location back into my house.

The following is an excerpt from the hypnotic regression of this event conducted by Yvonne Smith, CHT. at her office on March 28, 2008.

YS: Take a deep, deep breath and go to that time, that evening you spent at the Irvine Comedy Improv.

NL: I need to laugh because everything feels so heavy.

YS: Mm-hmm (affirmative).

NL: Reggie and I laugh all the time. He's like my brother. He's my cousin, but he's really like my brother. We get so silly.

YS: So you spent time with Reggie at the Comedy Improv.

NL: Yes. Now I have to go home and tomorrow is Saturday. And we'll go our separate ways. I parked up in the parking structure behind the place, the Improv, on the second floor, towards the front. My car is an SUV, the Saturn SUV. I have to go home, but I feel apprehensive.

YS: And why is that?

NL: I don't want to go forward. I don't want to get in the car and drive out of there for some reason. I don't know. Something's bothering me.

YS: Just try to get in touch with that emotion. Just reach deep inside. Get in touch with that emotion.

NL: I feel like I'm on the side of the road, and I'm getting out of my car. Someone's there. I'm being taken out of my car. I think my exit's up ahead. I'm was supposed to be going off that exit. It seems like whoever is here is really tall. I'm not sure, but taller this time for some reason.

YS: Does it feel familiar to you?

NL: Yes. He's at least as tall as me or a little taller. He seems different, though. It's dark out. I can hear cars in the background somewhere moving by. I feel numbed out, but I know that I'm not alone. There are other people here. Someone else is here.

YS: Do you know how many people?

NL: It seems like three. Three people. There's a field. There's a field on the other side of the freeway or something. Wow, I wonder. It feels like a light beam, something coming down, and there's a ship. But the ship you can't see, it's invisible or something. It's above my head, but it's low. It's amazing that you can't see it. There's a light, like a tunnel of light straight up, but you can't see the ship at all. It makes itself invisible. I don't know why anybody doesn't look or see this. It's 11:30 at night, and I don't know where the car got off, but it wasn't my exit. It was way before my exit.

YS: Where are you?

NL: Somehow I'm on the other side of the freeway. I think there's three of us and somebody else who's tall.

YS: There are three people?

NL: Three people.

YS: Do you recognize them?

NL: No. There's a woman with short, brown, kind of curly hair. She's standing. She's a middle-aged woman. I think she has glasses on. I don't know where the other one is. I think it's a man. I think it's a short man. But there's a field on the other side of the freeway, going to the ocean and that's where we're at. The grass looks crispy, golden under my feet like it's burnt from the sun. It's just an empty area between the freeways. I can't look up now, but I think we're going into that light.

YS: That's how you get in and out?

NL: It's a big hole at the bottom, a big round hole where the light comes down. I'm just not in the mood for this. It makes me mad. It all makes me mad. It really does.

YS: Why does it make you mad?

NL: Being bothered like this, because I'm just really tired in my life right now, just really exhausted. I need to rest, and this bothers me. It makes me angry that I have to deal with this.

YS: Do you tell them that?

NL: No, but I am so mad this time. I went out to laugh and to be happy. Now I'm standing on something metal. I don't know how we got in, but it's about standing in the light, and then you're there. There are one of those Tall Whites again.

YS: Where are you now?

NL: It's a saucer kind of craft. There's a centerpiece in the middle of the ship that has to do with propulsion or something. I realize it this time by looking at the way that it's built. Then you walk around in a circle on this thing to different compartments, but there's something in the center that makes this craft move and run. It's compartmentalized, separate from the rest. It's like you come in from underneath that area somehow, but now we're walking around. I think I'm moving my feet.

YS: Mm-hmm (affirmative).

NL: There are groups together for some reason. I can look around the table, and I see people with their heads hanging over, slumped over at this table. It's like a big rectangular table made of glass or metal. They're asleep, and I feel sorry for them somehow. I guess I feel different than them because I stay awake better.

YS: What else do you see?

NL: My hands are in my lap. I can look down and see the beveled edge. It's funny with the light in these tables, too. The light comes from someplace. You don't know where, but it's actually coming from the table itself. I think this is the first time there's a Tall White at the table across from me. The other one that shows up all the time and teaches me all kinds of things is the insect kind. He's sitting to the left-hand side, and he wants to show me off somehow. It's a weird thing. It's like I'm going to demonstrate something or be shown something. I don't know. There are some others around the table, too, besides the people that are slumped over. It's a pretty long table I think. There's someone at the head. So it's like a meeting to show things.

YS: What do you think they want to show you?

NL: I feel like they're putting ideas in my mind, in my head, wanting me to see something and remember babies. Remember and see babies, little babies in a room sitting on the floor on little pieces of cloth, and they look hollow and strange.

They move funny and look funny. Some have really big heads. Someone else is standing around like a nurse would, watching. But I don't think I'm actually there. I think the guy across the table is making me see this. There's babies on the floor, a bunch of them, like a dozen of them. There's a little one, small, staring at me. She's little, like a year and a half, just looking at me, and she seems much more petite than the others. I am remembering looking through a window at them.

YS: How does that make you feel looking at her?

NL: She's just so little, all by herself there. That's all. It makes me sad. You want to help them. She's sad all by herself. Doesn't feel warm at all in there, doesn't feel good. I can see a door that looks like a regular door, but I can't imagine a regular door would look like that there, but it looks like a door with a doorknob. It's right behind the one that I know, the insect guy. Right behind him, there's this door, and right next to him is the other guy that made me think of the babies.

YS: Okay. What else is happening?

NL: Now the door is opening, and I can see her standing there. Her shoulders are narrow, and her head is large. I don't see any eyelids, just these big eyes and a teeny, teeny nose with a straight mouth. She looks unhappy. They want her to walk out and come out to me. She does, and I think of the baby. I think of her as a baby. I think of her being that baby grown up. I really want her to look at me. She won't look at me.

YS: Why doesn't she look at you?

NL: I don't know. It's like she's just doing something she's supposed to do. I want her to look at me, and I want to jump up and hug her. She's just so sad, and there's no life. There's no life at all for her – none! It's like they don't fit anywhere. They don't mix, and they don't fit. They don't know what to do with themselves, because they're not normal. There's just so much sadness about them, it's awful. It's so sad and so hollow. You know that they've never had love. Anyway, I want a connection, but I can't get one. I can't get connected.

YS: Is she looking down?

NL: No, no. No, her eyes are just so sad, it makes my heart heavy. She just was doing what she's told like a little robot, and then she stood there for a minute, and now she's gone.

YS: Did she leave the area?

NL: Yes, she walked away and never looked back. (crying)

YS: I'm going to put a tissue in your hand.

NL: I never had children, and I wish I did. It's terrible when you never have a child of your own. It's so strange. You feel like you're connected, but you can't go near her.

YS: Mm-hmm (affirmative).

NL: She moves me so much. I want to know her. I think she's so beautiful. She's odd and strange and aloof, and I can't get near her. They have no life. What they do to them, the emptiness; they don't belong anywhere. They don't fit anywhere.

YS: Do they just live on the craft?

NL: Yes, yes. They have no place of their own, but they don't all live. Some are sick in that window, really sick. Some in there have heads so big they can hardly hold their heads up. It's a terrible thing. They're all like an experiment. Oh, these babies! It's the worst of any of it — the worst of the whole thing. You shouldn't do that to human beings. You can't play God!

YS: Do they tell you that you're going to see her again?

NL: Nobody said anything. I don't know. I'm tired of feeling like I'm less-than. I don't buy it anymore. Something is missing in them. We have something they don't. It's that emotional. I know it's crazy, and it needs to be controlled, but it's better than them, and that's why they can't leave us alone. Why would so many come to this planet? Why would they come here if they weren't fascinated with what we have and how we are? We have something they covet, and they want it. They're afraid of it, but they want the good part of it. That's why they try to take it from us to create it because they think they can get it that way. But the babies aren't getting it, and they aren't getting it because they haven't earned it!

YS: Okay, tell me what's happening now.

NL: I'm standing up, and I'm mad and yelling. I'm so tired of them thinking they're superior and they're not. They don't understand anything about our emotional nature. I want them to know how you can't just take it. You can't take it from us or make it. You evolve into it!

YS: And no one says anything to you?

NL: No. They're just watching me, letting me rant and rave, and now they've got the square over the table, the hologram, and that's it. That's what the emotions are. It's deep and multi-dimensional. You can't begin to explain it. We can hardly understand it ourselves.

YS: How do you feel about this?

NL: I'm never going to feel inferior to them again, any of them, ever, ever. We have a development in our soul, in our emotional side that they haven't even gotten near. I really understand something now. It's so clear to me that we are at the forefront of something new, entirely different. I had thought that we're lowly and they're so superior, but if you develop only in one area, you can miss the whole balance, and that's what they've done.

YS: What do you think they have missed?

NL: They've lost their speech. And yes, they communicate differently, maybe better, maybe not. They have the technology, and they can catch us and control us. They're trying to get what we've got by analyzing us in every single way, like what we feel, why we do what we do, why we're motivated, and why we dream. They don't do that, and that's what they want. I'm not afraid of them anymore; I'm just not.

YS: All right.

NL: I can see a young man with his head down on the other side of the table. I think they're taking turns with us and doing some different kinds of testing for some reason.

YS: Are you all in one room?

NL: We're in one room sitting at a long, rectangular table. I can see four people, on the other side, human beings. At the end of the table, there's someone that's not human. I don't know who's to my right, because I can't turn my head. I can't see. The others are unconscious because they don't want them to participate yet, or maybe they don't know how to stay awake yet. I don't know.

YS: Okay.

NL: Being mad is good when you're here. It makes
           you stay awake more too. I don't know what
           they're doing now. I feel like they want me to go.
           They're done with me. They're going to do things
           with those other people. I don't know what his
           name is, but the one that shows up all the time
           that looks like the bug, he's there too. He wanted
           me to come for this, whatever this is. I feel like
           he was showing me off for something. With him,
           you can't see feelings or facial gestures, but I
           think he does feel something with me, and he
           wants them to know that. They're done with me.
           They're going to go to somebody else next.

YS: Do they take you away from the table?

NL: I think I'm just going to go to sleep. I don't want
           to go to sleep. I'm all upset. I'm all excited. They
           just brought this tall guy in that looks like Clint
           Eastwood. God, I don't know what they're doing.

YS: Have you seen him there before?

NL: I have. I've seen him. We tried to hide once
           together in a room, but they found us. I don't
           know how I'm going to get home. It's
           really weird. I'm going to drive my own car
           home, but I can't remember driving my car
           home.
                        (End of Excerpt)

Alien Hybrid Nursery

Waiting in Line

I woke up abruptly at 4:44 a.m. on January 1, 2005, with the feeling that I had just been deposited back into my bed. I had gone to sleep the night before about 10:00 p.m., and while drifting to sleep, felt myself being transported through the air. I awoke in what looked like a small house that was dark. The floor seemed was made of wood, and I heard music playing in the background. There was a disoriented man in the room with me, and I realized that I had an abduction experience. They were forcing a screen image on me to make it look like I was in a traditional house. The moment that thought crossed my mind, the music stopped, and I lost consciousness for a few moments. When I was awake again, I saw that I was actually in a large warehouse, and the man was still with me. He appeared to be quite terrified, and I suggested that he find a place to hide. I knew they were coming, and I was having difficulty staying awake and focused.

My next awareness was of lying on a cold surface that may have been an examining table. The man had disappeared, and an ET was standing to the right of me, but I could not identify the species. My arm felt strange, so I glanced down and noticed a thin, inch-long scar on my forearm that had not been there before.

After another period of blacking out, I saw that I was back in the warehouse, along with the man who had been there earlier. He was still terribly frightened and mumbling to himself out loud. I tried to comfort him and suggested that he touch something metal. I had learned that touching metal could sometimes disrupt the energy they were using to control us. It helped to concentrate and maintain more awareness. I also told him that with practice, I had learned to maintain my awareness longer by fixating mentally on an object. I told him of an abduction scenario when I focused that I was able to stop a table from waving in and out of my vision. I have no idea how I learned these techniques for staying more alert.

There was another shift in consciousness, and now we were standing in a line waiting for something to happen. I could see that some of the people ahead of me had one or two ETs standing close to them. I wondered if they were there to control those people by keeping them in a foggy state through mental manipulation. I realized that, like everyone else, I was in line and waiting for my turn to sit in what looked at first like a dental chair.

The chair was made of smooth, solid metal and mounted on top of a pedestal base, rising approximately three feet from the floor. The back of the chair tilted slightly backward, becoming narrow at the top, and I watched a man being placed into the chair. The top of the chair projected several inches above his head, restricting him from any backward movement. The metal armrests projected outward from the side of the platform and were slightly longer than a human arm when fully extended. The cross design of the platform and the straps across the neck, wrists, and ankles restricted body movement and allowed easy access to the occupant's head, arms, and hands. The chair could also be lowered flat into an examination table.

Two figures then approached me, fading in and out of my vision, looking alien one moment and human the next. I wondered then how many extraterrestrials might already be among us on the planet using mass hypnosis like the underground device to cause us to see them as human.

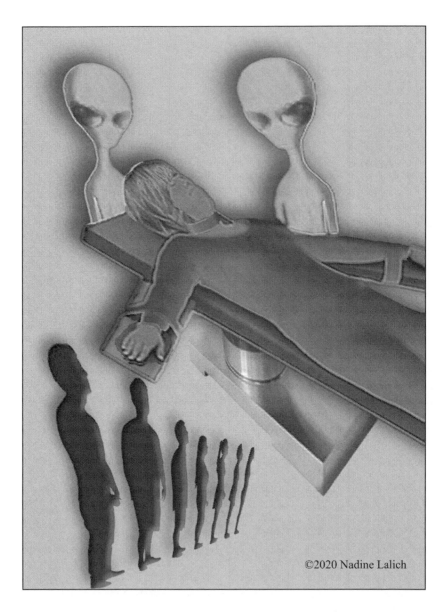

Implantation Chair and Table

At this point, three or four people were still ahead of me as I waited for my turn. I watched as another man was placed into the chair, screaming in terror, then saw three Greys working on his upper torso. I knew that I would also be placed in that chair soon, so I was surprised how emotionally detached I felt. When the time came for me to occupy the metal chair, I think they put an implant under into one of my back molars, and another black object into one of my hands.

In the distance, my brother suddenly appeared walking toward me from across the other side of the large room. They had staged these several times before, so I knew right away that it wasn't him. Whatever they were doing during this encounter, they certainly were messing with my perception again.

Locker Room for Humans

On June 15, 2005, I went to bed at 11:30 p.m. Later, I awoke to the sound of my dog, Murphy, shaking and whining. I sat up in bed and looked at the clock that illuminated with a background light; it read 1:11 a.m. I thought Murphy might need to go out to the bathroom, so I got out of bed and opened the sliding door onto the patio. He stepped out for a moment, but immediately turned around and came back in.

I was feeling uncomfortable and sat down on the edge of my bed, telling myself everything was okay. An uneasy feeling came over me that turned to fear when I began to sense a presence in the room. Then a strange buzzing sound filled the air, and I felt myself becoming dizzy. I quickly got out of bed again and went into the living room to turn a light on. I had read a book by Ann Druffel, *How to Defend Yourself against Alien Abduction*, and I decided to try one of her suggestions for stopping an abduction. I felt foolish, but I retrieved a can of hair spray from the bathroom and sprayed the contents around the house. Frustrated, I gave up and decided to lay back down. Murphy, still shaking, jumped up on the bed and snuggled close to me for comfort.

I woke up again at 3:30 a.m. with a clear memory of having been in a locker room. There were a lot of other people coming and going with most looking dazed. I could see three identical adjoining rooms, each with rows of dark green or grey lockers with benches in front. I remembered worrying about where I was supposed to place my belongings and where they were going to have me lay down. Human men and women continued to come into the area slowly, all of them looking like they were in a stupor, only partially conscious. The only other aspect I could recall was seeing an ET in a red uniform who appeared to be supervising the event.

©2020 Nadine Lalich

Locker Room for Humans

Human Locator Disks

I was living in an apartment in Lake Forest, California, when I awoke the following morning with a detailed, conscious recollection of having had an ET contact the previous evening, April 8, 2006. I remembered stepping outside onto my patio, where I observed a gold light in the sky, moving fast and zig-zagging directions. Suddenly the electricity in my apartment, as well as some areas around the complex, went out. I went back inside and tried to find my cell phone and a flashlight, but it was too dark for me to see anything.

I was anxious and went back onto the patio several times to look up in the sky. Within a few minutes, several cigar-shaped crafts appeared high in the night sky. I noted that one had thrown out a beam from the front end of the ship that shone down onto the ground in a circle. I could also vaguely see many small objects exiting the larger crafts then dropping through the air. Debbie, a colleague of mine at the time, unexpectedly appeared at my front door. I told her I knew that the ETs were here and coming our way. The electricity remained off.

Shortly after that, we heard the sound of a commotion outside. I opened the door again and saw people in their nightclothes standing along the walkways of the complex. Suddenly, a round disk about 8 inches wide came flying through the air, bounced off the door, and came to rest on the ground alongside the front of my apartment. I thought it was a piece of paper, but upon a closer look, I realized it was a disk made of metal. A nickel-sized hole pierced the center, and it had strange black symbols etched into the metal, and several notches cut into the edge of the disk. For some reason, I thought that it might contain information specifically related to me. I believe disks like this one were what I had seen dropping from the sky. I wondered if they used them to locate abductees during mass collections, and I remember kicking the one at my feet before I stepped back into the doorway.

The small group of people dressed in nightgowns and robes was pressing together and getting closer to my apartment. I wondered if the ETs were trying to gather us into a group so they might pick us up all at once. I did not want to go!

Someone came to the doorway where I was standing as if expecting me to come out, but I was mentally resisting. I could see that the group of people had passed my door and were now continuing down the sidewalk toward the back of the complex, which was a wooded canyon. I realized that the person standing in front of me urging me to go might be an alien controlling everyone's perception to more easily control the group. By this time in my life, I had had enough of these experiences that sometimes I could sense when they were manipulating my awareness. That is especially true if they try to project themselves as a human because their movements become quite robotic. At this point, Debbie was standing behind me in the doorway, extremely upset, and saying she needed to get back to her family. I also began to wonder where my dogs were.

My next memory is of standing just outside my front door, and I was alone. I could still see the crafts in the sky, but now they were hovering lower to the ground. I lost awareness for a time, and when I regained my awareness, I found myself in a corridor that looked like a waiting room. Two other vaguely familiar people were also there waiting for something. As I had so often thought in the past, it occurred to me again that disguised extraterrestrials are probably living all over our planet now, perhaps even concealed as human children.

Craft in this area.

Lower Apartment

Map Data: Image ©Google, Digital Globe

Lake Forest, California Apartment Abduction

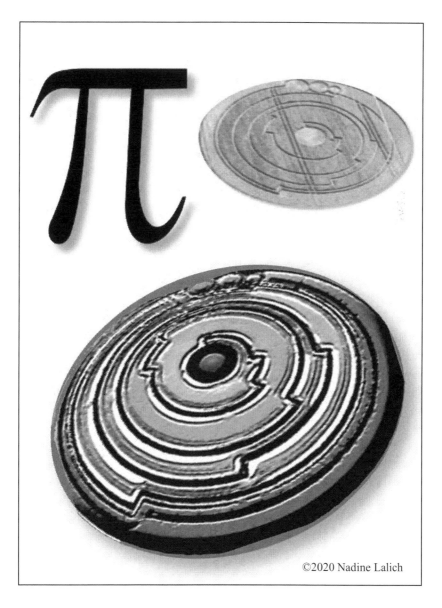

©2020 Nadine Lalich

Human Locator Disks

As I waited in the corridor, I felt somewhat weightless, as though I was immune to the pull of gravity and could have levitated if I tried. I stretched my arms out and lunged my body upward to test my theory. I did, indeed, feel myself lift from the floor a bit. I wondered if I was in a location in space without normal gravity. As I was pondering this question, I experienced an overwhelming sense that my psychic powers had increased.

The waiting was over when the end of the corridor opened into another room. I found myself standing in a large open area that looked much like a warehouse or airport terminal, with many humans and aliens moving about. There were dozens of counters like the checkout stands in a grocery store, and it looked as though they might be using them as intake counters. Overall, dozens of humans were in line at each counter, being interviewed and physically examined. More aliens were traveling about the room, generally in groups of two. I was confused because some of them seemed to be moving their mouths as if they were talking! This was the last thing I could remember before I woke up in my bed. It was still the middle of the night.

The next day I went to work and decided to approach the woman who had appeared in my experience the night before. I barely knew her, so I had to be cautious about broaching the subject in my work environment. I went to her office and prefaced my remarks by telling her that I had a strange question to ask. Being a pleasant person, she was open and responsive, so I asked her if she believed in UFOs. She paused a moment before replying and then said it was funny that I should ask that. She went on to say that she had experienced a bizarre dream about UFOs the night before, and had discussed it with her husband and children at breakfast that very morning. She added that she and her family had never talked about aliens or UFOs before. I found her remarks quite intriguing.

I was especially curious about the disk that landed at my door during this experience. After some research, I learned that it was the symbol for pi. A few years later, when I began compiling the material for this second book, I learned that the identical design had appeared as a crop circle at Barbury Castle, Wiltshire in the UK on June 1, 2008. Retired astrophysicist, Mike Reed, stated that the geometric pattern clearly showed the first ten digits of pi, the ratio of the circumference of a circle to the diameter:

> I noticed a photo of the Barbury Castle pattern. It shows a coded image representing the first ten digits of Pi - the ratio of the circumference of a circle to the diameter. The tenth digit has even been correctly rounded up. The little dot near the centre is the decimal point. The code is based on ten angular segments, with the radial jumps being the indicator of each segment.[7]

Pi has countless applications beyond geometry and trigonometry. For example, it can help scientists to understand objects and phenomena in nature, which contain circular shapes, such as the orbit of the planets, the concentric waves created by a stone falling into a pond, or the way light and sound waves ripple. How that information pertains to these disks, I cannot fathom.

---

[7] Daniel Bates, "Easy as pi: Astrophysicist Solves Riddle of Britain's Most Complex Crop Circle," DailyMail.com, (June 17, 2008) Accessed October 1, 2019, https://www.dailymail.co.uk/news/article-1027178/Easy-pi-Astrophysicist-solves-riddle-Britains-complex-crop-circle.html.

I received the following e-mail in 2010 from a man who described having seen similar disks in his experiences.

> Date: January 25, 2010
> From: J.C.
> Re: The Information Disks!
> I finally see some corroboration of something I once witnessed – amazing! This is the first time I have ever encountered anything in this field about "information disks," as I found on your website and in your book. I have read Whitley Strieber and other authors, extensively, but nobody had anything on the flying information disks.

I found another aspect of the experience on April 8, 2006, particularly interesting. For many years, I had been wearing a small triangular device on a chain around my neck called the "Q-Link." It is a copper coil that hypothetically influences the biofield of the human body by allowing the electromagnetic field to recuperate more quickly after exposure to EMF fields. One of the manufacturer's claims was that it relieved some of the symptoms of Fibromyalgia. Having been diagnosed with that condition some years before, in 1991, I purchased a unit. Within a few weeks, my symptoms reduced somewhat, so I continued to wear it. During this experience, one of the Greys exhibited an interest in the device. He reached out and grabbed it, then held it in his hand for a few seconds before letting it drop.

Dr. Beverly Rubik, PhD., an advisory panel member of the National Institute of Health, described the biofield and the possible effects on the human body from wearing a Q-Link in her paper, "The Biofield Hypothesis: Its Biophysical Basis and Role in Medicine."

Biofield: the complex, extremely weak electromagnetic field of the organism hypothesized to involve electromagnetic bio information for regulating hemodynamics. The biofield is a useful construct consistent with bioelectromagnetics and the physics of nonlinear, dynamical, nonequilibrium living systems. It offers a unifying hypothesis to explain the interaction of objects or fields with the organism and is especially useful toward understanding the scientific basis of energy medicine, including acupuncture, biofield therapies, bioelectromagnetic therapies, and homeopathy. The rapid signal propagation of electromagnetic fields comprising the biofield, as well as its holistic properties, may account for the rapid, holistic effects of certain alternative and complementary medical interventions….[8]

The following is an excerpt from the hypnotic regression conducted by Barbara Lamb on July 16, 2006, regarding the event that transpired on April 8, 2006.

BL: Today's date is July 16, 2006, and we're focusing on an experience that happened previously, going back to the night of April 8, 2006. Nadine, we're going to go back to your vivid dream or actual experience of seeing many large UFO's in the sky overhead that was releasing many smaller ships, and to whatever other details followed seeing those ships. To do that, we're going into a nice

---

[8] Beverly Rubik, "The Biofield Hypothesis: Its Biophysical Basis and Role in Medicine," Journal of Alternative and Complementary Medicine," (July 5, 2004) Accessed October 18, 2019, https://www.liebertpub.com/doi/10.1089/10755530260511711.

state of deep relaxation. What is your first awareness that something unusual is happening?

NL: I hear a sound at the front door of my apartment, a knocking sound, or clicking. Nothing has ever happened at my front door like this before. There's some commotion going on outside, and I have a strong sense that I'm supposed to go out there. I'm outside now, in front of my apartment, and standing barefoot on the cement. Trabuco Canyon drops way down just ten feet in along my apartment building, and I can hear something down there, making a sound in the canyon. My neighbor lady is here, too. She's in a nightgown, without her glasses on. She usually wears thick glasses, but she doesn't have them on now, and she seems out of it. I'm feeling fuzzy, but I know there are ships up there.

BL: Can you see any ships?

NL: When I walk out on the sidewalk and look up, I can see an object in the sky. It's pretty low and hanging over the canyon at the back of my apartment. It's a matt grey color, not shiny. Oh, I'm in the ship now!

BL: So, you're not on the ground anymore?

NL: No, I'm on the ship and standing in a room with only females, female humans. There's a lot of us standing around in our nightgowns or nightclothes. Everyone seems pretty out of it with their arms hanging down at their sides. This experience has something to do with babies and war, taking care of babies at a time when there will be a big war. They're showing us smoke and bombs. I wonder if they will rescue Earth's babies at a time of war.

BL: What else do you sense?

NL: They have altered the DNA in some of these Earth babies. They have added some of their own DNA into them to change the human race and get rid of the aggression. Only some of the babies are going to be saved from the planet when the disaster comes. The extraterrestrials alter their DNA when they're inside the pregnant mother by injecting their DNA into her womb with the baby inside. We are the protectors of these babies.

BL: Okay.

NL: Oh, there's something wrong. Three races of extraterrestrials are here right now, and one of them is a Reptilian race. I think there's something wrong with them, and maybe they're dying. I can see different types of beings in various types of ships. The Reptilians have cigar-shaped crafts. The little Greys and the Big Whites with the big heads are here, too. Are they dying, too?

BL: Did they tell you who will be dying?

NL: They're telling me that their cells are dying because they have exposed themselves to conditions here that are different from their environment. They might have to mix their cells with human cells to survive here for long. Right now, they can't stay here for very long at any one time. They take the blood from the babies who have been genetically altered, and they inject it into themselves so they can stay here physically for longer. They need some ingredients from our immune system to be okay here. They're telling me that this is a time of urgency now. Someone, a big white one with a big head, is close to me now and looking right into my eyes to see the information I'm gathering. It feels like when they're looking through me, they see inside my brain.

BL: Describe more how that feels to you.

NL: It makes the back of my head feel like a screen, and he can look through my head as if looking through a tunnel into my mind to see the screen in the back of my mind. You know, I have always had this weird ability myself, to stand before the screen at the back of my mind and write information on the screen. Then I can look at the screen later to remember the information I had written down. I've done this many times.

BL: Does this experience of him looking into your eyes seem familiar to you?

NL: Oh, yes, familiar. He's looking at stored information units, but they can't see or know my intention because it's not stored in the same way.

They can't understand anything that's tied to emotion, and intention is tied to emotion. They can't grasp the concept of a loving God or love or compassion, in general, the way we can. They watch it happen in our minds, but they can't grasp it because there are different structures and receptors in our human brains that allow emotion and connection. The extraterrestrials don't have these structures so that they can only see the objective information in my mind. Sometimes I think that if we weren't so scared when they look into our eyes like this, we could even see information about them in their eyes.

BL: Are you afraid of the white one who's looking into your eyes now?

NL: Well, not exactly because my perception of them has changed over time. My favorite beings are the bugs that look like a grasshopper or a praying mantis. They do a lot of research and testing, and they remind me of laboratory assistants. There are four different kinds of beings working together at all times. Man, I don't know where all these thoughts are coming from right now. They just come up so fast. Maybe they're putting these thoughts in my mind.

BL: That's okay. Just stay with the experience. Is there anything else going on?

NL: These beings are interested in the coil that I'm wearing around my neck as a piece of jewelry, the Q-Link. They know I wear it for more control, to keep them out, and they're not comfortable with it. They're just looking at it. One touched it briefly. I've been in this room before, and I know this whole experience is an exercise to see if we're ready for when the time comes. Things are going to escalate, and they'll reveal themselves when the chaos comes, so we'll be more receptive to them.

BL: Can you see anything else? Are they showing you anything about that?

NL: They showed me a future when they're landing and registering huge numbers of people, but it hasn't happened yet. It's only a future possibility. If it does happen in the future, I'll react more quickly and effectively because I've been previously exposed to it. I need to come back to Earth now. I have mud on my feet. I must have walked down into the canyon with bare feet, and now I'm up out of the canyon, and I'm outside my apartment. It doesn't seem like I was gone long, maybe just thirty minutes or so.

BL: How are you coming back? How do they bring you back?

NL: I've been getting back by floating onto the patio on a beam of light. The door back here isn't open. The dogs are asleep. I'm getting back into the apartment through the glass patio door somehow. Wow, I'm thirsty, and I'm drinking water with my hand from the bathroom tap.

(End of Excerpt)

The New Men in Black?

On January 20, 2007, MUFON Orange County was hosting a talk featuring Lynne D. Kitei, M.D., a physician, UFO researcher and author of *The Phoenix Lights*. I was fascinated by the Phoenix Lights incident when vast numbers of people in the Phoenix, Arizona area had observed a massive craft moving across the night sky. My friend, Chris, also had some interest in the subject, so he agreed to meet me at the Costa Mesa Library, where the meeting was being held.

We arrived early and seated ourselves at the back of the room along the far wall where a single row of chairs had been placed. Our position against the wall gave us an easy side view of the dozen or so rows of chairs facing the podium. The last two of these rows were directly in front of where we sat.

Most everyone was seated, and the meeting was about to begin when two strange-looking men entered the room. They were slender, six feet tall, and looked to be about thirty years old. They were dressed identically in all black - jeans, hooded sweatshirts, and even black tennis shoes. Their hoods were pulled down over their faces, and they each wore very dark sunglasses. From what I could see of their faces, I could tell that their skin was very light in color and without facial hair. They appeared tentative and stopped to glace about and survey the room. Then they moved slowly toward the last row of chairs, walking in a jerky and synchronous manner while maintaining shoulder-to-shoulder contact. They sat down in the center of the very last row facing the podium, directly in front of where Chris and I sat along the wall.

Meeting Room where Men in Black Arrived

Within a few minutes, the room was quite full, and I noted that no one sat in their row nor the one in front of them. As the meeting progressed, I found it odd that all of the people who were seated in the four rows directly in front of them were asleep in their seats.

Over the next two hours, I felt compelled to study the two men, so I kept my eyes in their direction much of the time. Twice during the announcements before Dr. Kitei spoke, the men stood up in unison, clapped a few times, and then immediately sat back down, resuming their original position. While seated, they rarely moved and faced straight ahead without shifting in any other direction. They never removed their extremely dark sunglasses, nor spoke or looked at one another during the entire time. The only communication that I noted was the exchange of strange hand gestures. Sitting beside me, Chris agreed that their behavior was very odd.

Halfway through the meeting, there was a break, and the two men stood up and stiffly walked outside into the courtyard where many people had gathered. We followed them and saw that they had retreated into the dark shadows of a corner of the building. They remained there for the entire 15-minute break without speaking to anyone.

Chris left shortly after that, and I decided to stay and take a photo of the two men. I was back in my original seat with my phone in my hand when I became so overwhelmed with fear could not. Instead, I stood up and walked behind them in the last row and took a picture of them from the back. Then I left the room and went to the bathroom.

In the restroom, I was feeling shaken, so I decided to leave the meeting early. I went back to the main hallway and headed for one of the two doors that led outside to the parking lot. As I neared the door to my right, I saw that one of the men was now standing directly outside that door, blocking me from pushing it open. I quickly turned around and headed for the door on the other side of the hallway. There I found that the second man had also positioned himself directly outside that door, preventing me from going through! The meeting was still in progress, and no one else was in the hallway or the dark courtyard leading to the parking lot. I went back into the meeting room and sat back down. A minute or two later, both of the men also came back to their seats, but at no time did they ever look at me. I waited another ten minutes before bolting from my chair and almost running to my car in the parking lot.

One might suggest that these two men were only trying to have some fun by dressing and behaving bizarrely. If that were the case, surely, over the two hours I observed them, they would have altered their behavior to some degree. If it was a joke, could two young men be able to maintain the identical body position and movements for such a long time? Would they be able to remain entirely solemn and emotionless for that length of time? I also wondered why no one sat anywhere near them, and why all the people in front of them fell asleep. Why would several men in charge of the meeting with whom I spoke acknowledge the odd behavior, but not approach them at least for security reasons? Could these two figures have been a new, more updated version of the Men in Black? While attending a Ufology conference two years later, I met a man who traveled with Dr. Kitei during many of her lectures. I spoke to him about the men, and he told me that similar figures had been seen at many of Dr. Kitei's talks in the past.

The New Men in Black?

The Visitor from 1950

On July 25, 2008, I attended the MUFON International Conference in San Jose, California. I flew up from Southern California with a friend, Cathy, to host a book signing table. In the hospitality room for vendors and speakers, my table was located directly in front of the entrance.

At about 1:00 p.m., I took a break from the table to attend one of the lectures while Cathy staffed the table. I returned about an hour later to find my friend looking wide-eyed and shaken. She told me that while I was gone, a bizarre woman had approached the table several times, demanding to speak with me. Cathy described her as being quite tall and thin, with behavior that was aggressive and intimidating. She also found it difficult even to look at her.

I had just sat down in the folding chair next to Cathy when Craig Lang, the late hypnotherapist and Assistant State Director for MUFON Minnesota, came over to chat with me for a few minutes. I was sitting back down when the door to the hospitality room opened, revealing a strange-looking woman standing in the doorway. Once she spotted me, she strode quickly to my table and leaned over me dramatically. Both Cathy and Craig drew back instinctively, but I sat frozen in her gaze.

The woman was at least six feet tall, extremely skinny with long thin, bony arms and an impossibly narrow waist. Her 1950 style clothing was somewhat shabby, and in the crook of her bent arm was a tattered leather purse. Wavy straw-colored hair cut to chin length, framed her long face, and pointed chin. Most mesmerizing were her piercing, amber-colored eyes that bore into me, sending fear racing along my spine. I was frozen in position, unable to move or look away from her while she leaned menacingly over me firing questions, one after the other. "What did I know about

Reptilians? Had I ever seen one? What extraterrestrial races had I met, and where did I see them? What were my intentions for writing a book? Did I know anything about defense contractors and what they were up to?" She spoke fast in an angry tone and a high, sing-song kind of voice.

I knew it was ridiculous, but as I sat suffering her onslaught unable to move, the thought occurred to me that she wasn't human! Was she a Reptilian? After about two minutes of suffering her barrage of questions, I was able to shake off the paralyzing mental fog and stand up. As I did, she leaned back into place on the other side of the table. Dry-mouthed, I could barely stutter back at her that I knew of Reptilians, but nothing about defense contractors. She continued to rant on about what defense contractors were up to and that they should be stopped. After repeatedly insisting that I knew nothing about defense contractors, she became quiet and awkwardly strutted back through the door.

Cathy and Craig were still beside me, motionless, also apparently suffering some degree of physical and mental restraint. In silence, we watched her through the side windows of the room as she entered the parking lot and disappeared from view. After a few moments, we spoke briefly about the high strangeness of the event. Cathy and I both remained nervous that evening in our hotel room, fearful the woman might return.

The Visitor from 1950

5
FAMILY HISTORY

Over the years, claims of alien abduction have been made by multiple members of the same family line, from one generation to the next. People who have experienced the phenomenon tell of instances where their parents or children also describe experiences involving the Greys and other ET races.

My grandfather, Thomas Lalich, along with three of his brothers, emigrated from Austria to the United States in 1901, entering through Ellis Island. Several years later, he moved to Wisconsin and finally settled in the upper peninsula of Michigan, where my father, also named Thomas Lalich, was born.

My father was a most unusual man. Incredibly creative and talented. He possessed a photographic memory, and, according to the Army Air Force, where he had an IQ over 150. During World War II, he flew 52 missions in a B25 in the Mediterranean theater, serving as a radio operator and waist gunner. Later, he taught radiotelegraphy and electronics at Scott Field Army Air Forces Technical Training Command.

©2020 Nadine Lalich

The Crew of a WWII B-52 (T. L. Front Left)

Tom's Nighttime Excursions

Unfortunately, Tom had post-traumatic stress disorder from the war and also from a genuinely traumatic childhood during the Great Depression. As a result, his social skills and the ability to relate to others was poor. He was most contented when spending his free time alone, working on projects in his basement shop. He also spent much of his life immersed in books, satisfying a voracious appetite for learning. His interests included science and technology, foreign language, astronomy, mathematics, and much more. My brother and I were intrigued by his intellectual capacity, but also put off by his many peculiar ways. To cope, we often tuned him out, especially when he offered lengthy discourses on abstract theories and concepts. As teenagers, we would sometimes shake our heads and roll our eyes when he would make bizarre comments such as, "I wish they would come back and take me off this planet," or "I know I don't belong here."

Many years later, after processing my own experiences, I reflected back on his strange remarks. I also recalled the stories his three sisters shared with me about things that took place in their childhood home in Ironwood, Michigan. On numerous occasions during the mid-1920s through the 1930s, one or more of his siblings would find Tom standing in front of a second-story window, nonresponsive, in a trance-like state. Sometimes before they could stop him, he would step out onto thin air and disappear moments later! Usually, someone in the household would go outside to look for him, but always without success. In a few hours, he would return without any memory of the event. Clearly uncomfortable about these episodes, my aunts proclaimed that he must have landed each time standing up, directly on his feet, which would account for why he was flat-footed!

Ironwood, Michigan Home

Aunt Patricia and the Men in Black

There was another strange tale told to me by my mother's sister, Patricia. Among my seventeen aunts and uncles, she was the most intelligent and scholarly. Although we had been close all of my life, she never shared this story until after my first book about extraterrestrials was published. While visiting at her home, we were discussing for the first time the alien abduction and UFO phenomenon when she told me of an incident that occurred during 1950 while she was living in Dearborn, Michigan.

On that unusually cold winter morning, there was a knock at her front door. With the storm door securely locked, she opened the heavy front door to see who was there. Much to her surprise, standing on her porch were two very odd-looking men dressed in black suits and wearing fedoras, and a black car was parked in her driveway. Although they were wearing sunglasses, she could see that their skin was a whitish color. They spoke in a strange robotic voice and insisted that she let them in the house. Although startled, she was not one to be bullied, and she slammed the door in their faces.

As she watched them from the window, she noticed they moved in a strange and jerky fashion. They repeatedly walked up and down the sidewalk, along the driveway and back onto the porch. A notable aspect of the encounter was a terrifying sense of dread and physical discomfort that came over her throughout the experience. She did not observe them disappearing, but my aunt did say that after spending fifteen or twenty minutes, they abruptly disappeared.

6
ET DESCRIPTIONS

The following summary is a brief description of the entities I recall having seen at some point in time during my paranormal contacts.

Tall and Short Grey

Short Greys have appeared many times in my experiences over the years. They have large, slanted black eyes, perhaps covered with a membrane. They are capable of doing a mind scan of a human brain by merely looking into a human's eyes, presumably for obtaining information from that person. They conduct most abductions and physical examinations, sometimes along with a Tall White or Reptilian present. They move in robotically as if connected in consciousness and seemingly without individual volition. In most cases, they do not express emotion, communicate solely telepathically, and rarely engage in lengthy two-way communication. However, there have been several instances when I did sense an emotional awareness from what I believe was Tall Grey female. In another experience with a Tall Grey female, I received a direct, telepathic response to a question that I posed in my mind, "Do you find humans repulsive?" Her curt reply in my mind was, "Yes."

The Tall Greys have appeared only on a craft or during a military experience, usually functioning in a supervisory capacity managing groups of humans. They have also appeared dressed in human-type uniforms.

Tall White

The Tall White species has appeared numerous times in my experiences as a supervisor during physical examinations or training sessions. I have also observed them standing in front of control panels on a saucer-type craft or in an examination room. They have presented only as males, with an attitude of superiority and a sense of disdain for humans. They dress in long, white or beige colored robes or tunics with long sleeves.

Reptilian

Reptilians have appeared during physical abductions and in underground caves or bunkers, often supervising and controlling activities. They emit a strong odor, and their skin is grey-green with the texture of a typical lizard. They appear very strong and muscular, over 6 feet tall, and wear a metallic armor on their chest and sometimes legs. Their demeanor appears threatening and warrior-like with predatory sexual overtones. They seem to be able to shape-shift or, more likely, may be able to disguise their appearance through manipulating a human's perception.

Insectoid or Praying Mantis

The Insectoid or Praying Mantis extraterrestrial is quite unattractive physically. In my experience, I have only encountered one being who has been present in numerous scenarios. This being who I believe was male seemed to possess a degree of emotional awareness, a tremendous curiosity, and an affinity for humanity. This particular individual seemed to be specifically assigned to me for a mental evaluation, testing, and training. During abduction events, I have observed him collaborating with Tall Whites and Short Greys.

Hybrid Child and Adult

During my thirties, I had what I initially considered to be normal, reoccurring dreams. Each time I would be sitting on a chair in a large room with people positioned along the walls watching me. I could never get a good look at them where they were in the shadows, but I imagined they might be relatives. Next, I would be presented with a small child about three or four years old who I believed I was supposed to interact with. The child was always barefoot and clothed in a sleeveless dress made of a course, beige material that hung to the middle of her calf. She always looked unhealthy with poor skin and thin, blonde hair. She evoked within me intensely sad, maternal feelings, and I felt fiercely protective of her. I would even be drawn to tears, simply remembering these dreams.

Years later, during what were ET experiences, I was introduced to an adult female Hybrid who I strongly suspected was the same child from my dreams grown to adulthood. Considering the passage of time between when I saw the child in the dreams, and later, when I saw the adult female Hybrid, it might be possible. It is also possible that the meetings with the child may not have been dreams at all, but took place during ET abductions. When meeting the adult, I experienced the same feeling of profound motherly love that I had when I met the child. During later contacts

171

with the extraterrestrials, they inferred that she had, indeed, been created partly from my genes. My overall impression of this Hybrid as a child and adult was that she was depressed and unhappy, living in a controlled environment on a ship in space with little or no power to direct her own experience.

Stocky Elf

The Stocky Elf appeared only once as a positive influence when I was a ten-year-old child. The being was a male who seemed intent on helping me by dissipating an enormous amount of negative emotions that was making my life quite difficult. Although this encounter was brief, it left me more balanced and tolerant of my life circumstances. The being was quite stocky and muscular, standing about four feet tall with pale skin, a broad forehead, and pointed ears.

New Men in Black

Although they did not appear as typically recorded Men in Black wearing a black suit and fedora, the two male figures that attended an Orange County, California MUFON meeting on January 20, 2007, may have been a newer version. Like the traditionally described Men in Black, there was a strong sense of negative energy about them that aroused fear and aversion. Also, like all Men in Black that have been described, they dressed in all black and wore sunglasses over their pale, white faces. Instead of a suit and fedora, they wore hooded sweatshirts with the hood pulled down, covering much of their faces. They also displayed robotic movements that were identical and in sync. While sitting for several hours in the meeting, they neither spoke to anyone nor each other, but communicated only with strange hand signals.

1950's Woman

This female, standing at least six feet tall, was dressed in somewhat ragged, out-of-date 1950's clothing. Her manner was aggressive, mesmerizing, and frightening. She was also obsessed with defense contractors and the Reptilian race. During the one time I encountered this being, I was overcome with the feeling that the skinny woman who walked with an awkward gait might not be entirely human, and perhaps might be a Reptilian in disguise. When she pressed her face close to mine to interrogate me, her piercing eyes glimmered with an odd amber color, and it was the first time I ever recalled hearing a voice quite like hers. I was astounded by her remarkable ability to mesmerize three people making it nearly impossible to turn away.

7
METHODS OF CONTACT

Over the many years that I have experienced the ET abduction phenomenon, the contacts have taken place in a variety of ways. The following descriptions are solely based upon my own experience and not meant to suggest that others experience the phenomenon in the same manner.

Conscious Physical

In these instances, the contact or abduction took place while I was fully awake and aware, as in my experience in 1991 in Sedona, Arizona, when I was taken from a parked vehicle. I have experienced other events awake and standing while preparing for bed, and during the middle of the day while driving in my car.

Sleeping Physical

This kind of contact would begin with me waking up in my bed during the middle of the night. I would be overwhelmed with the feeling that a craft was overhead and that they were coming. Often I would also sense or even vaguely see a figure in the room near my bed. The experience would proceed from that point with my realizing that I was paralyzed and sometimes a feeling that I was floating upward. I believe that these contacts may be actual physical abductions.

Lucid Dreaming

There have been many instances while sleeping when I have been engaged in a common dream. Suddenly, there would be a shift, and I would become more awake and lucid as if I was actively participating in the event. Although the proceeding dream scenario would totally unrelated to UFOs or aliens, extraterrestrial beings would suddenly appear and engage with me in a manner quite similar to all abductions, i.e., examinations or testing on a craft. It may be possible that these kinds of events may escalate to a physical abduction, or they might be an interaction taking place within my consciousness alone.

Regular Dreaming

These events have occurred as regular dreams that involve ships and aliens from the very beginning. The sense that it is only a dream is present from the beginning, and the scenario unfolds in fragments as though my mind is simply trying to process the phenomenon.

Sleeping Astral

This type of contact occurs when I am sleeping in a bed during the night, and I wake up sensing that contact is about to happen. I can feel myself rise from the bed but do not feel that my body has been taken. During one experience, I recall being quite awake and alert as I felt myself rising upward. As I looked back down, I could see my body still lying upon my bed. Another time, when I also felt quite alert and conscious, I felt as though I was being carried in a clear glass tube or vessel by three or four extraterrestrials along an underground walkway. I could see clearly outside of the container, but I felt terrified when I realized I could not see my own body. We passed several beings who were standing together on a walkway, and they glanced up as though they could see me. Overall, it was a very confusing experience.

Conscious Telepathic

This kind of experience always begins with seeing the repeating numbers of 1111 or 444. In either case, I am fully awake and engaged in some common activity when I feel a strong impulse to stop what I am ding and look around me, particularly toward whatever digital clock may be in the area. The repeating numbers will be showing on the clock, and I will fixate upon it for up to 30 seconds. During that time, I have a sense that information may be being uploaded or downloaded from my brain and consciousness. Then, as abruptly as it started, it stops, and I go back to whatever it was that I was doing before I was interrupted.

8
TRACES OF CONTACT

Nose and Ear Bleeding

Occasionally, after physical contact, I have noticed varying amounts of blood on my pillowcase. Upon closer examination, I would find traces of blood inside my nose or my ears, and sometimes in both areas. On one occasion, I also found a notch in the helix area of my outer ear that looked as though a piece of skin and cartilage had been clipped away. This area continued to bleed off and on throughout the following week.

Location and Position Changes

During some instances, when it appeared that a physical abduction had taken place at home, I would find myself waking up in a different location from where I had gone to sleep. There have also been times when I awoke with the memory of an event that I would also find my body in a strangely contorted position.

Lost Time

An example of a particularly distressing lost time event took place during the middle of the day in 2004. I was working for a law firm in Newport Beach, California, and left the building by myself around noon to pick up some lunch. About 3:00 p.m., I awoke to find myself sitting in my car parked on the side of a road that was miles away from where I worked. I was in an unfamiliar area with no memory to this day of what occurred. My employer noticed and commented, wondering what had happened to me.

Ear Ringing, Clicking, and Hissing

Before a contact one or both of my ears might begin ringing, and if I was in bed, I might also hear a pronounced clicking or hissing sound in the room or feel a buzzing sensation in the air. An interesting article appeared on the World Health Organization website that described the effect of electromagnetic frequencies on the human body.

Radar systems detect the presence, direction, or range of aircraft, ships, or other, usually moving objects. This is achieved by sending pulses of high-frequency electromagnetic fields (EMF). Invented some 60 years ago, radar systems have been widely used for navigation, aviation, national defence, and weather forecasting....

Exposure to very intense pulsed RF fields, similar to those used by radar systems, has been reported to suppress the startle response and evoke body movements in conscious mice. In addition, people with normal hearing have perceived pulsed RF fields with frequencies between about 200 MHz and 6.5 GHz. This is called the microwave hearing effect. The sound has been variously described as a buzzing, clicking, hissing or popping sound, depending on the RF pulsing characteristics. Prolonged or repeated exposure may be stressful and should be avoided where possible.[9]

Many abductees also describe hearing similar sounds before an ET abduction. Perhaps EMF technology is being employed by extraterrestrials during abductions, or perhaps humans using the technology might also be involved.

Inability to Stay Awake

During the 1990s, when experiences were happening quite frequently, there were instances when I was alone at home, completely awake and moving about, that I would suddenly become intensely drowsy. It was so extreme that I would feel like I was about to fall over, and if I sat down, I would instantly fall into a deep sleep. Sometimes I would awaken to find myself in a different location of the house with one or two hours have passed. There might be fragments of a memory of contact or no memory at all, but the experiences always troubled me and left me fearful.

Lights and Electromagnetic Disturbances

Occasionally, before or during an experience, electricity in my house would go out, or static electricity would be present. On several occasions, I recall seeing a variety of lights

---

[9] World Health Organization Staff, "Electromagnetic Fields and Public Health: Radars and Human Health" [Fact Sheet No. 226], World Health Organization, Accessed October 29, 2019, https://www.who.int/peh-emf/publications/facts/fs226/en/.

outside or in a room or craft. They included round white or colored lights and straight white beams that were coming from an object in the sky. I recall one event when a glowing ball of light about two feet in diameter appeared outside my bedroom window while I was preparing for bed. Suddenly, it moved into the room and exploded into a shaft of light, filled with bluish sparkles. Whenever the experience involved being on a craft, the entire area would be filled with indirect white light. Those occasions when I was being tested or trained on alien devices, a soft blue light would emanate directly from the equipment itself.

Scoop Marks, Scars and Punctures

In some instances, after an ET contact, I would find physical marks on my body. They have included a scoop mark below my right knee, thin straight scars on my forearms and back, and puncture marks on my right shoulder in the shape of a triangle. Most of the sites would disappear within 24 hours, except for the pronounced scoop mark or indentation that was located just under the skin in the center of where the triangle puncture marks had been. To this day, it remains.

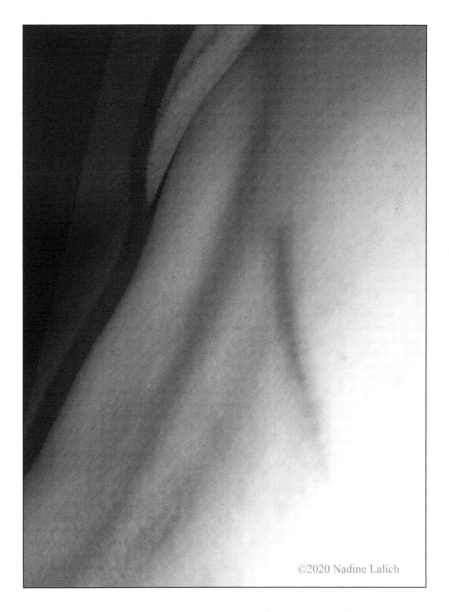

©2020 Nadine Lalich

Mysterious Scar Discovered Upon Waking

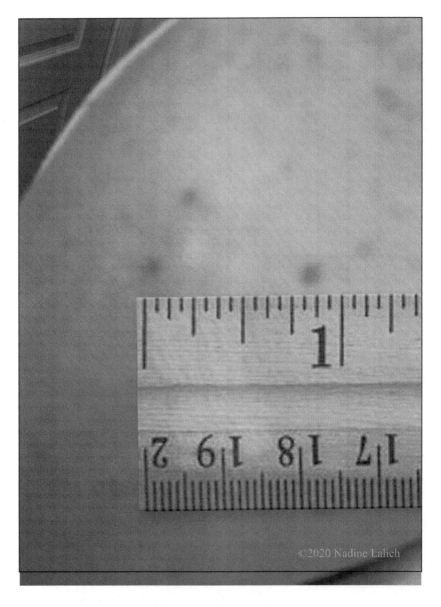

Triangle Puncture Wound, Right Shoulder June 10, 2018

Compulsive Nighttime Driving

In the early years, subsequent to my June 1991 abduction, I would sometimes become overwhelmed with an irresistible urge to leave the house at night to drive to a remote location. Certainly, I would question the thought, especially since it was usually accompanied by a sense of foreboding However, there were occasions when I did succumb to the urge, but I do not have any conscious memories related to those excursions, nor were any hypnotic regressions conducted back to those events.

PTSD and Anxiety

Admitting to myself that I might be an alien abductee was probably the most difficult thing I have ever had to face. My sense of reality was shattered, and I faced the monumental task of trying to incorporate the bizarre phenomenon into my daily life. After the first conscious awareness in 1991, my sense of safety and security were shaken. My orderly and predictable life had come to an abrupt end. For the next thirteen years, as I endured in silence and secrecy, I suffered occasional flashbacks to that event and suffered periodic bouts of anxiety triggered by another experience. Sleeping was difficult as many experiences took place at night. I began to check closets, behind doors and car seats, and even added locks to my bedroom door. I avoided anything to do with the subject of UFOs or aliens because I refused to accept the extraterrestrial hypothesis, holding out for a more logical explanation. Eventually, I turned to every spiritual tool I had developed over the years. I also employed odd techniques and advice from the only UFO book I had read up until that point. It was titled, *How to Defend Yourself against Alien Abductions*, by Ann Druffel.

I found her suggestions to be somewhat questionable, but I was open to trying anything that might stop the experiences that were tormenting me:

A ninth technique that holds out considerable promise is Repellents, which can be defined as the use of herbs, essential oils, flower essences, and specific substances such as salt and iron....In my database, several resisters state that metal objects help ward off greys...Another method of using metal objects...bar magnets or metal crosses.[10]

---

[10] Druffel, Ann *How to Defend Yourself Against Alien Abduction*, Three Rivers Press, New York (1998)

9
MIND CONTROL, MEMORY AND CONSCIOUSNESS

Many experiencers would agree that during an abduction, the extraterrestrials use a mental technique or other technology to calm us and alter our perception. Considering the volatile nature of our race and the terrifying prospect of alien abduction, employing some method to subdue and control the subject would make sense.

When evaluating ET contact, I believe there is always some degree of distortion in memory that has to be considered. Speaking from my personal experience, although my conscious memories seem to unfold in a reasonably orderly fashion, they are nonetheless fragments of memory separated by blank, unconscious periods; therefore, it would be difficult to confirm the actual order. Even with effort practiced over many years, it has been impossible for me to maintain my awareness during an ET contact for very long before I would lose consciousness. I can estimate that I have been able to maintain my awareness for up to five minutes, but I would not be able to guess the amount of time that passed after being rendered unconscious.

There are other things I consider when evaluating my memory of an ET event or that of another person. Could past experiences influence how I perceive the new experience? Are there any motives or expectations showing up that might color the situation? Is religion or another type of training or conditioning affecting how the memory is stored or interpreted? For example, someone with a strong religious point of view might consider a non-terrestrial life form to be an angel or a demon. Are emotions, fantasy, or ego affecting perception?

In some of my own experiences, I am stunned by the extensive amount of conscious memories that I can recall, and it leaves me baffled as to their true nature. In those instances, the only thing I am confident of is the fact that I experienced an extraordinary paranormal event, the nature of which I may never fully understand. On those occasions, when I was fully awake and lucid at the time an experience began, such as the Sedona event, I am more confident about my ability to evaluate the incident. I try to keep an open mind and to refrain from making hasty judgments. We, humans, are out of our league in dealing with this phenomenon. We have little to no control over what is happening, so I place my attention on actions that offer a small sense of control over the circumstances. Those include practicing to improve my awareness during contact, managing my emotions better, and continuing to make written records and drawings of an event as soon as possible afterward.

For clarity, a picture can be worth a thousand words. To that end, using an old film clip, the following illustration demonstrates how I imagine my brain might record memories under various circumstances. The top row of the film represents how my mind might record an ordinary memory when I am awake and fully conscious. The next line suggests how my mind could record an event when I am drifting in and out of sleep. The third line shows how my brain might record an ET event as it is taking place, in pieces or fragments, with blank sections for those moments when I am rendered unconscious. Finally, regardless of whether or not you consider regression hypnosis to be a useful tool, a competent hypnotherapist can help to retrieve additional information from the subconscious mind that could assist in creating a more cohesive depiction of an event.

Memory and Recollection

Complete Recording of Event

Recording of Event while Drifting In and Out of Sleep

When someone falls in and out of sleep while watching a movie, recollections can be sharp, fuzzy or blank.

Consciously Recorded and Recalled ET Event

Conscious memory of an ET or MILAB event is saved and recalled like puzzle pieces, in a seemingly orderly fashion, but with blank spaces in between.

Hypnotic Regression for Recollection

Regression hypnosis, allows the person to step into the blank spaces between the puzzle pieces of memory, expanding understanding of the event.

©2020 Nadine Lalich

Memory Recording and Retrieval

10
MILITARY ABDUCTIONS

In 2006, Barbara Lamb and I agreed to co-author a book about alien abduction. The book would include a portion of my story and case summaries from 24 other abductees who she had worked with. To choose which ones we would include in the book required me to review 100 files initially. I was, of course, shocked to learn of the many similarities between cases involving people from all walks of life, but none of these cases mentioned the military in their experiences. The field of Ufology was new to me, and I was not at all familiar with military abductions, commonly referred to as "MILABS." In 2001, I did have one conscious memory involving military personnel, but on top of all the other ET experiences, it was too much to bear.

Shortly after *Alien Experiences* was published, and I began to speak at the public level about my experiences, the MILAB phenomenon returned. Sometimes they looked like ordinary soldiers or officers, but I also saw enhanced soldiers with a more massive physique who looked identical to each other as if they had been cloned. These encounters with military-type personnel would commence in the middle of the night, often after midnight. Sometimes the contacts involved just humans in military uniforms, but other times humans and ETs appeared to be working together. There were also instances when it seemed that humans, aliens, and human clones were collaborating. Overall, the MILAB encounters were quite unlike any of the alien abductions.

First of all, these events unfold in a way that indicates they are real events taking place in the third dimension as we know it. People enter and move physically through the rooms of a building through regular entrances. Transport is provided via silent, black helicopters primarily, although there have been instances when disk-shaped crafts were also present.

During MILABS, I have memories of being transported to an underground and underwater base, and of being physically examined while being in a hazmat unit. They conducted interrogations with one or two people at a time by having us respond to questions by pressing pictures imprinted on a computer screen while military personnel observed through a viewing window in an adjacent room. To induce sedation or conduct psychological manipulation, they injected or had us inhale drugs, and once also used an unusual audio device to promote a semi-conscious or unconscious state.

Unlike ET contacts, communication is strictly verbal, and telepathy is not employed by military personnel, although it may have occurred on one occasion with an alien who was also present. I also recall seeing unusual crafts under construction and situations when humans and extraterrestrials were working together on an aircraft.

Over the past six or seven years, I took a break from actively pursuing Ufology and shifted my focus to other areas of my life. I found the development of the military aspect in the phenomenon nearly as difficult to accept as I initially did the existence of alien life. With the publishing of this book, I am happy to say that I am now coming to terms with the probability that some humans may be cooperating with extraterrestrials here on earth, and that our government may be involved. Whether or not there is a connection, I am happy to report there have been far fewer ET experiences and no conscious recollections of new MILAB experiences during this period.

The Winnetka Event

The following is a conscious memory of an experience that transpired on November 15, 2001, while I was living in Winnetka, California. I had awakened from a deep sleep the previous night but a sound I could not identify. I got out of bed to investigate and flipped the switch on the small lamp mounted on the wall over the nightstand. The light would not go on after several attempts, so I assumed the bulb had blown out. My husband then woke up and tried the lamp on his side of the bed. That light would not work either, so we assumed the electricity had gone out. He got out of bed then and tried several wall switches in the room to no avail.

I then went to the window that faced the front of the house and looked into the dark sky. There were a few clouds and many stars visible. A movement caught my eye, and I saw a huge ship approaching our neighborhood with several smaller crafts flying alongside it. I was excited because I thought it would finally be an opportunity to introduce my skeptical husband to the UFO phenomenon.

I grabbed my bathrobe while yelling for him to come outside to the front yard, which he did. By the time we were out, the large craft was directly over our house, and I began to feel somewhat foggy. The large ship was mostly cylindrical in shape, with the front and back sections more rectangle. I could see windows along the front section and lights at the tail end, and I wondered if it was a military transport helicopter. The smaller crafts that had remained high in the sky looked like little boomerangs, and I had the impression they were protecting or acting as scouts or observers for the larger craft.

I could sense that something was going to happen, and I felt both excited and agitated as I waited. Standing on the sidewalk, I noticed other people in the neighborhood had also come out of their homes and were standing in nightclothes and moving along both sides of the street. I tried to speak with my husband about what was happening, but he seemed to be in a stupor. He was mumbling about not seeing anything and would not acknowledge me.

Two houses away, I saw a light coming from the craft that was now hovering low to the ground and lowering a large metal basket about ten feet long sectioned into a dozen or so compartments like an egg crate. Farther down the street, I saw more baskets being lowered to the ground by a similar craft, and I wondered why I had not seen them before.

I turned to look in the opposite direction and saw that one of the baskets had landed on the ground directly to the right of me. A figure that I think was a human male was standing alongside the basket wearing tan coveralls, gloves, and a hood of some kind over his head. In his hand, he held a pencil-thin, foot-long metal rod with a small round apparatus at the end. I could hear him talking to me, but I wasn't sure if it was vocal or in my mind.

"You're married, aren't you? Then you have to come with me. It's time."

I thought he planned to use that instrument on me in some procedure, and I wondered if he thought I was pregnant. I did not want to go with him, and I considered that he might really be an alien disguising himself. If that were the case, why was he so human-looking? Also, why would an extraterrestrial be wearing coveralls with a hood and gloves that looked like a sterile laboratory outfit? What I was sure of was that I did not trust him. I lost consciousness then. My next memory was of being back in the house. My husband was already there sitting on the couch in the living room, but still in a semi-conscious state. I tried to get his attention and sat down beside him, upset and crying profusely, but he would not respond.

I have another fragment of a memory related to this event. I was feeling highly agitated and standing on the deck of a huge ship that was docked somewhere on the coast. I looked up into the sky and saw the same craft I had seen earlier over my house now flying low and overhead of where I was standing.

Helicopter with Basket for Transporting

Underground Military Base

This experience took place during the middle of the night on October 3, 2008, while I was living in Laguna Woods, California. During this event, I believe I was taken from my bed, although I do not remember the actual abduction or transport. I do vaguely recall entering a large metal door into a mountain and then clearly recall going down a cylindrical, glass elevator with a tall military-type man. As we descended in the elevator, I could easily see several large open floors that looked as though they had been carved out of stone and earth. Along the sides of each layer were metal grid walkways mounted to the walls with staircases going downward. Here and there, I could see blue, double doors at the end of the corridors.

One of the floors housed an unusual gigantic craft where many people in uniforms were working. They stood on the floor or on scaffolding that surrounded the craft. Although I viewed the area from quite a distance away, I had a strong impression that not all of the workers were human. They were all of a similar height and wearing the same tan overalls, but they moved differently. As we continued to descend, I also noted that the air was heavy and quite difficult to breathe.

Door to Underground Base

©2020 Nadine Lalich

Underground Glass Elevator

Underground Base Showing Craft and Walking Tunnels

We had passed below the floor where the craft was when the elevator stopped. Without speaking, the man escorted me onto a metal grate walkway and through a long tunnel that had a set of blue doors at the end. We went through those doors and into another tunnel that led to more blue doors. Eventually, our walking ended at a second glass elevator. Going down one more floor, we ended up in an enormous chamber, much larger than all the previous levels. The dark, damp cave had small spotlights stationed along the dirt floor and rocky walls, and in the distance was a huge two or three-story building that looked like a mansion made of big blocks of concrete. I also realized by then that the man escorting me was a replica of several other men we had passed along the way.

My next recollection was of being in the building and standing in a room with rows of large rectangular tables. I realized I was not wearing my nightgown, only underpants, so I tried to cover myself with my arms while I looked for my clothing. All the while I felt that someone was watching and following me. I pulled back a curtain and saw a lot of people looking very busy, but they didn't pay any attention to me. Behind the curtain were more long tables with clothing stacked in piles, some of it dirty. None of it looked like mine, so I grabbed a long shirt to cover up.

My next recollection was of standing in the large foyer of the building. I was impressed again with the fact that it looked like a luxury mansion or hotel. A beautiful wooden staircase located rose impressively from the right side of the room and curved to the left onto the second floor. My escort was still with me and guided me into a room off to the left side of the foyer that looked like a typical doctor's office. A man came into the room dressed in a white lab coat who seemed to be a doctor. Strangely he kept fading in and out of my vision, sometimes not looking human, and I knew he

Cloned Human Soldiers

wanted to talk to me, sedate me, and get information from me. I was sitting on the end of an examining table when he suddenly stepped away and went through a doorway into another room at the back of the office.

Instantly I jumped off the table and left the room, ran through the foyer and out the big double doors at the front. Outside it was dark, and I ran around to the side of the building. The structure had regular windows, and I looked in to see if I could tell where the doctor had gone. The light was on in the room, but it was empty.

I made my way along the side of the building, hugging the wall tightly until I reached the back. Peeking around the corner, I saw large sliding glass doors that opened onto a concrete patio with a section that extended out perpendicular to the building another ten or twelve feet. That portion looked somewhat like a runway for clothing models. I could see several figures standing on the patio and through the open doors, others who were inside the large room. Some of them were extraordinarily tall, wearing tunics and robes that draped to their feet. They did not appear to be humans. Overall, the scene looked like a social event with dining and relaxing.

A few moments later, I heard voices and saw a half dozen men making their way from the front of the building toward me. In the distance, I also saw a small area cordoned off with plastic fencing, and I headed that way to hide. Inside the enclosure, the ground was muddy with shallow pools of water scattered about, and tiny plants and moss were sprouting from the marshy ground.

They quickly found me, and several of the identical-looking men brought me back into the building to a room adjacent to the foyer. I remember saying to them, "Whoa, I don't believe it. That is so amazing. You look exactly alike." They did not respond, and I heard someone in the room tell them to keep me quiet or knock me out.

They set me down in a straight-back chair in the center of the room with the doorway to my back, and I was no longer able to move my body. In front of me were two black leather lounging chairs with full arms. Although I could not turn my head, I could see from my peripheral vision that there were several large dark screens off to my left and right that looked like flat-screen televisions. I heard people talking behind me, but I could not see them. They were discussing the prospect of taking me away from the facility. It occurred to me that they were engaged in something significant, and I pleaded with them to let me stay. I found my attitude toward the situation quite strange because, previously, I had always wanted any experience to stop.

Two females then walked over and stood in front of me. They were wearing white robes that fell to the floor and a covering on their heads that limited my view of their faces. Nonetheless, it was evident that they were not human. The people standing behind me had decided to remove me from the area. I could see from the corner of my eye the original person or ET who had been in the examining room, and he was speaking out loud, saying he had made up his mind not to give me another chance. Again, I pleaded with them, "Please, I will cooperate. I want to know what's going on here. I want to be a part of this."

I still felt reasonably clearheaded when two of the male guards sat down in the leather chairs opposite me. They put on huge headphones that nearly covered the entire sides of their heads. I think they were intended to block whatever sound waves they were going to expose me to. Suddenly, I could feel my consciousness fading out, and the room began to dim and look far away. I remember feeling strong determination and telling myself to remember everything! Don't forget anything! This is very important!

This experience was one of the more lucid I have had. From the moment we entered the underground facility until much later, when I was rendered unconscious in the underground building – it felt like a real experience. I was curious about the audio technology they used, so I did some research on the psychoacoustic effect on humans by infrasonic, sonic, and ultrasonic frequencies. The following excerpts from a 1998 Marine Corps newsletter posted on the website for the American Federation of Scientists, read:

> Non-lethal weapons, such as acoustic and directed energy weapons, can provide Marines with an alternative way to deal with noncombatants...and still accomplish set objectives and missions. Non-lethal weapons are defined by the Department of Defense policy as discriminate weapons that are explicitly designed and employed to incapacitate. ...
>
> Another item being looked at is a directed energy weapon that uses low-frequency soundwaves that can knock a person out but causes no permanent damage.[11]

In further researching the current use of sound waves for brain stimulation, I found the following excerpts from an article written by Antoine Jérusalem, Professor, Department of Engineering Science, at the University of Oxford:

> At the moment, non-invasive neuromodulation – changing brain activity without the use of surgery – looks poised to usher in a new era of healthcare. ...

---

[11] Sgt. Jason J. Bortz, "New Weapons Provide Alternative for Marines Dealing with Non-Combatants," Marine Corps News, (August 28, 1998) Accessed January 11, 2020, https://fas.org/irp/news/1998/08/980828-usmc.htm.

But what happens if this technique for altering our brain waves escapes regulation and falls into the wrong hands? Imagine a dictatorial regime with access to the tricks and tools to change the way its citizens think or behave.... How dystopian could it get? I can see the day coming where a scientist will be able to control what a person sees in their mind's eye, by sending the right waves to the right place in their brain....

This technology is not without its risks of misuse. It could be a revolutionary healthcare technology for the sick, or a perfect controlling tool with which the ruthless control the weak. This time though, the control would be literal. ... I am also convinced that human nature is such that if something can be done, it will be done. The question is by whom.[12]

Underwater Military Base

This experience occurred on April 14, 2010, while I was living in Laguna Woods, California. I awoke in the middle of the night with the feeling that someone was in my bedroom. My dog, Annie, was standing on the floor at the foot of the bed and acting strangely. I tried to raise my head but realized that I was paralyzed and unable to sit up. I remember being taken from my home with a blanket wrapped around me and then placed into a helicopter or similar craft. Shortly after that, I believe I was transferred to a second ship that soon was flying north along what I assumed was the Pacific coastline.

---

[12] Antoine Jérusalem, "Mind control using sound waves? We ask a scientist how it works," World Economic Forum, (November 7, 2018) Accessed October 29, 2019, https://www.weforum.org/agenda/2018/11/mind-control-ultrasound-neuroscience/.

Suddenly, there was a hard jolt, and in the row of small round windows in front of me, I could actually see water splash against the windows. I was astounded by the feeling that we seemed to be traveling under the ocean. The only other conscious memory I had of this experience was of being in a hazmat unit and being tested while military people watched. On October 23, 2013, Barbara Lamb conducted a hypnotic regression back to the date of this experience on April 14, 2010.

BL: I'm going to count down from number ten down to number one. And when I get down to number one, you're going to be there now, beginning in your room, in your bed on that particular night, April 14th, 2010. On April 14th, 2010. You are at your home, and you are sleeping on your bed. Eventually, you will be finding yourself awakened. Let's go to your first awareness of this on April 14th, 2010, while you are sleeping in your bed. When you're aware of something, just mention it out loud with your words.

NL: Annie, my dog, was on the floor, standing up at the end of the bed.

BL: Okay, is that unusual for Annie to be standing up like that?

NL: She's looking at something. Acting strangely, but not barking.

BL: Okay, she's just looking. Which direction does she seem to be looking?

Aerial View of Laguna Woods MILAB Abduction

NL: Towards the bottom of the bed. The right side, by the window, and there's a dark figure there.

BL: Okay, there is a dark figure?

NL: A dark figure you can't see. She's just looking at him.

BL: Okay. So she seems to be looking at the shadow.

NL: And there's a light behind it from the window.

BL: Okay. And you see it too? Okay. All right. The light behind it. Now, does it seem like that's coming through the window from outside? Or is it emanating from inside, somehow?

NL: The light's from a sidewalk light, coming through the curtain. There's a big black figure standing in front of the bed. That's what she's looking at, but she's afraid. She's not even barking. It looks like a man.

BL: Okay.

NL: He has a cap on.

BL: I know Annie's not barking, but do you see anything?

NL: There's someone in the doorway of the bedroom. Someone's in my house. It seems like people. There's another man.

BL: All right. Is he just standing there without moving?

NL: The second man is standing in the doorway, waiting for something. Instructions. I can't move. I'm cold. I'm trying to move. I can't move for some reason.

BL: Mm-hmm (affirmative).

NL: I can't sit up or anything.

BL: Are they aware that you can see them?

NL: It's all secret. No one is talking. They're waiting for the next thing. It feels like a helicopter. It's like a helicopter outside.

BL: Do you hear it?

NL: I'm in my pajamas. I'm in a nightgown. And I'm outside.

BL: Oh, you're outside now.

NL: And someone's taking me somewhere.

BL: Now, where is this helicopter in relationship to where your house is?

NL: It's by my garage somewhere. It's quiet. I don't hear anything. There's no sound.

BL: Wow.

NL: There's no sound from it, nothing.

BL: Take a really good look. I realize it's night time, but take a good look at that helicopter and describe what you see.

NL: From a distance, it looks like a helicopter, but when I get closer, it's round, and it looks kind of silver. It fades in and out and then almost looks like a helicopter. Then I get a feeling of a rounded bottom or something. It's different. I don't know what it is, exactly. It's confusing.

BL: Do you actually see the big helicopter blades?

NL: No. That wouldn't make any sense at all. It can't be blades. It's not big enough there. No blade.

BL: So you, if you look at the top of this object, whatever it is, where the propellers would be, you don't see them?

NL: It's flat, and nothing's moving, really, up on top. Maybe it's not a helicopter, but it seemed like there was something on the ground that was a helicopter. Now it looks like there's something overhead, hovering over the parking lot area, maybe 25 feet up. Not far. It's just sitting there.

BL: Not moving or anything?

NL: It is not moving, no. Someone's pushing me up towards it. I just had this feeling I was being walked out and up into this helicopter. Now it feels like there's this thing overhead now, not that far up. Its more like an oblong or a cigar-shaped ship maybe. Something like that, but it's up off the ground, like twenty feet, or something.

BL: Okay.

NL: I think it's by the garage, but a little farther out. It seems quiet. Everything's quiet. I can't tell, but I might be covered with something. I don't know what, but something is wrapped around me. I don't even remember going out the door. All I know is that I'm just suddenly on the side of the house here.

BL: Mm-hmm (affirmative).

NL: I'm on the side of the house going towards this helicopter or something up there. I'm going up there. Yes, it feels like something dark is wrapped around me that is so I can't see or make any noise.

BL: You said that something is wrapped around you. Did you mean it's wrapped around your head, too?

NL: My body.

BL: Just your body?

NL: My body. It's different, whatever this is.

BL: What are those men doing at this time? Can you tell me where they are?

NL: I know there's one to the right of me, and maybe more on the left. They've got these caps on their heads and matching pants and shirts. It looks like dark green or gray. A real dark uniform with a hat and it's got a brim. They're very matter of fact, the way he talks to me.

BL: Okay. At this point, is it accurate to say that you can't move?

NL: No, because my feet are moving, and I can't resist now. I'm moving along with them because they hustle me along, sort of. At least along the sidewalk, with one of them on each side.

BL: Do you feel the ground under your feet as you're moving?

NL: No. I don't physically feel much of anything.

BL: Okay. What about the temperature outside?

NL: I think it's cold. I think that's why I've got a blanket on. I'm going somewhere, somewhere by the water and the ocean. I'm on the ship now.

BL: The craft?

NL: On a ship. In a craft. It's round. I'm going somewhere. I don't know why there's water. I feel like there's water, and we're by the beach, going north by the ocean.

BL: So you have a sense that you're heading north?

NL: It is heading north. Yeah. It doesn't look like a helicopter now. There's this thing in the middle of the room that you can put your hands on or something. It's round. There are two people ahead in front and rows of chairs. The round thing in the center is like a core in the middle of the ship, and something round goes up from it.

BL: Is it like a column?

NL: Like a column, but the bottom part comes out of the room more like a ledge around it. The pillar goes up and, I don't know why, but I keep thinking people put their hands on it for some reason.

BL: Do you see somebody with their hands on it right now?

NL: Two tall people, but these aren't people. They're not really people. They look white, very tall, and lanky. There are two of them doing something to this tall column. I think I'm sitting in something on one side of the column, and somebody is behind me watching me. I feel sedated and unable to do much. I'm physically drugged, sort of. I'm going somewhere with water. I don't know why this has to do with the ocean. Wow!

BL: Are you able to see out of this vehicle, or whatever you want to call it? Can you see out and see if there's water out there?

NL: On the edge, in the upper half, there are some panes of some kind that you can see out of, and I can look out.

BL: All right.

NL: I have a feeling we're going into the water. I feel like we're going into the water.

BL: Now when you say that you are going into the water, how do you know that?

NL: We're splashing into the water.

BL: Does that mean this whole thing that you're sitting inside?

NL: The whole thing. The entire ship's going in. It's going into the water!

BL: All right.

NL: It's like a jolt's hitting it.

BL: Does the whole object that you're inside of feel like it's moving?

NL: You can feel it hitting the water and going into the water. Yeah, then it's, I don't know. It's a different feeling afterward. It's like a vibration I can feel.

BL: Are you seated on something?

NL: Yes. It's curved. And kind of [inaudible] by a curve.

BL: Okay. Are you reasonably comfortable sitting there? Is this thing moving in the water?

NL: Anxious. Anxious.

BL: Are you feeling anxious?

NL: I've never done this before. I've never done anything like this before.

BL: Oh, yes. Okay. Okay, now, as all this is going on, do you have any awareness of those people who are there?

NL: There are these two tall people on the pole, and two people who are not people are in the front, in two curvy chairs. The windows up front are on top, so when we hit the water, it got dark in those windows.

BL: Okay.

NL: Someone's to my left is talking. They're talking in vocal words.

BL: Do you hear the words with your ears?

NL: With words. Audible. Using voices. Someone is also standing here, to my right, right behind my chair, with a uniform on.

BL: Okay, now, with the one who's talking with an actual voice, can you understand what's being said?

NL: I can't really hear words, but they're talking to someone else that's not in uniform, that's not fully human. There's three talking, talking about somebody else coming to join them.

BL: Okay.

NL: Someone else is coming. They're preparing for somebody to come. We're going there, and someone else is coming.

BL: All right. Take a good look now.

NL: The one that doesn't look entirely human, I don't know what he is, but sort of like a man.

BL: Is he standing upright, two-legged, like a man?

NL: Yes, very tall. Over six feet and wearing some other kind of material. Something shiny and silky or something.

BL: Are you talking about his clothing?

NL: Mm-hmm (affirmative). He looks dignified.

BL: And what about his face?

NL: Chiseled, kind of.

BL: Chiseled how?

NL: Not like the two on the column. I don't know what this is. I've never seen one of them before. They're kind of Oriental looking, but I don't know what they are.

BL: Is there any hair on this one?

NL: There is some hair on the head, I think.
        I don't know what. It's facing sideways from me.

BL: Is it the profile?

NL: It's the side of the face. And my head's turned the wrong way. I can't move, but it looks like he understands what the others are saying.

BL: Mm-hmm (affirmative).

NL: I don't think he's saying anything, though.

BL: What is it that gives you that impression he's not fully human?

NL: I don't know. Maybe it's his energy or something. I don't know what it is. Or his skin color. It's white. I can only get it out of the

NL: corner of my eyes. My head can't turn around and face him. I get Oriental and some kind of hair on his head with high, high cheekbones from the side.

BL: How about his eyes. What do they look like?

NL: They're big, but I can't see them well because it's only the side of his face. So I can only see just this corner of it., but it looks like his eyes would be big. And his face is kind of flat in the front — kind of flat.

BL: Is there a nose sticking out?

NL: No. No.

BL: Is there any nose at all?

NL: Not much. A bump, maybe? There might be a higher collar in the back on the back of the shirt that he's wearing. They're still in conversation getting ready for somebody coming. Okay. There's a hangar on the bottom, under the water. Yes, there's some kind of a hangar underwater that you go into.

BL: Okay. How are you able to see that?

NL: We're there now, somehow.

BL: Are you there now?

NL: I don't know if I went to sleep for a while. I don't know. It just seems like we're here now in this thing.

BL: Okay.

NL: There's a cement floor with water on the floor. This thing we're in has got legs on it. It's got legs on it, and that's how it stands on the floor when it goes down. Water's dripping from things in there where we're standing. Now they're taking me somewhere. I see the bubble, the big bubble. And a built-in office or a building at the other end that's enclosed, but there are doors you can go through. This giant, giant room that everything is in looks like metal, a big metal room that's round on the top. It's all like metal with a flat bottom. I don't know how they got this thing in there, but they did. And there's another bubble inside the main one that's big and clear.

BL: So this other bubble is one that you are going in yourself?

NL: I'm not going in now. I'm walking somewhere else.

BL: Now, are these men right there with you as you're walking?

NL: One man is taking me somewhere. There's a way to get into that second bubble. In the bubble, you can see an opening from outside.

BL: Now, did you have to get out of your own craft, in order to be walking toward that bubble?

NL: I would. Yes. I think it opens on the bottom, and you come out of the bottom somehow. It's like there are big pillar lights that come out of this craft, and then it opens, and you can come out.

BL: Okay.

NL: It's different. This is different from any experience I've ever had. This doesn't make any sense. Totally different. I feel like I've been put into some kind of smock or dress outfit like an examining gown. It's white, or pale blue and it goes all the way down to the middle of my legs. There is someone else there. They're doing this to somebody else, too. We both have these big smocks on.

BL: Do you think that person has also been brought there?

NL: Yes. It's a man. And they're bringing us both into this room with a table in it. I don't know why, but I think they want me to talk to a psychiatrist. It's weird.

BL: Now let's just....

NL: And it's like being on display.

BL: Are they taking you into this other bubble?

NL: I've already been there. There's a room that leads from the bubble where you get changed. Then there's a nurse in there, and you put this thing on.

BL: Uh-huh. A changing room sort of?

NL: Yeah. She's like a nurse. I think she takes your temperature, but I don't know what else she does, exactly. I don't feel afraid, just curious. I think the nurse is just a woman, or she looks like a woman.

BL: Like a real human woman?

NL: I think so.

BL: What about this other man? Does he seem to be human?

NL: Yes, and he acts as if he knows me. I think this has happened to him before. He looks like he's 40 or 50. He's older and his hair is dark. It's combed to the side, and greasy. He's got a rebellious attitude. When he spoke, he told me, "Don't say anything. Don't say anything to them." It's like he knows how to do this thing and we shouldn't talk. There are things on a table. We're supposed to be in a show or something and going to be asked questions. We're going to do tests and show things and push buttons. Someone is observing us and following us from outside and going to watch us. They're testing us for something.

BL: You and the man?

NL: Yes.

BL: Is he being tested, also?

NL: Yes.

BL: Is he saying anything?

NL: They want to know what we know. There's another man that speaks slowly to you with words. We're speaking words in here. It's not telepathy. And he's slow and patient, the way he talks to ask you questions. "What do you see? What do you think? What do you know?" Like that. He writes notes on some kind of electronic device in his hand like a tablet. There's somebody outside that he can talk to and ask questions through the glass.

BL: How does the air seem to you in there? How's your breathing going?

NL: The air is cool, damp, and heavy. I don't know who this other third person is in the room with us. I thought it was a psychiatrist and a man. I don't know who that is, but it may not be a man.

BL: But he seems to be watching and testing you?

NL: Watching and testing, yes. They want to know stuff, and we're going to tell them, but they don't want it by our voice. They want it by things we push. We answer differently. Mechanically, there are some things in front of us, and we push a button. I think that this guy maybe is not a psychiatrist. I am talking out loud to this other man in here with me, but with the doctor guy, it may be telepathy after all. And we listen to his telepathy, and then we push the buttons — something like that. We push things.

BL: Are they giving you instructions?

NL: Yes. Then we answer by what we push while other people watch from outside.

BL: Have you seen this before? Do you know what you are supposed to push?

NL: I'm just answering with lots of yes and nos. Some things are colored like buttons that are red and black. There may also be some monitors stuck on me, sensors, or something stuck on me.

BL: Okay.

NL: He's at one end of the table, and I'm here with a console on top of this table. It has these wedges that we push, and that's how we give our answers, our responses to whatever they ask us. But I think it's telepathy he's using when he asks us things.

BL: Rather than speaking out loud?

NL: Right. They want to know more stuff like, "What did you see? Where did you go? How many times? When did it happen?" Those kinds of things. Questions like that.

BL: Okay. Does it seem like you know the answers right away?

NL: Yes. Yes. Where we've been and who we've seen. What were they doing? What did their ship look like? Who else was there? How long were you there? What things did you see? Equipment? How did you feel? How do they make you calm?

BL: Did it seem like they're asking about regular events in your everyday life?

NL: No, no, no. No, they want to know what contacts, what ET contacts you've had, who you've seen. How many times. What did they look like? What did they wear? What did they want? How did they treat you? How many times? Are they in your house? Where did you go? How many kinds at one time?

BL: Specifically about extraterrestrial contact?

NL: Yes. How does it move? How does the ship move? What do they ask me? What do they want from me? What do they do to me?

BL: So these things that you're pushing, these button types of things. Do they have letters on them or words on them? Or symbols of any kind?

NL: It might be more like a console like a computer. You just push a button when you see things that you relate to. Instead of saying, "Yes," you push one that looks like what you've seen. Like that. You push the things you recognize, what you've seen. All your answers are more pushing with your finger.

BL: So there are pictures or scenes?

NL: Yeah, like pictures, and you're just touching it.

BL: Okay. Are these pictures like what we'd see on a computer screen or television screen?

NL: It's a flat thing, like a computer screen, a panel that's set in front of you. They keep changing it, and different pictures come up. When you answer those, another set of buttons shows up. You push the ones that are, yes, you've seen, and that you identify.

BL: Okay. Now, what is your reaction to all this? Any particular feeling about having all these questions asked of you?

NL: It makes sense to me. I understand what they're doing, why they're doing this. It really makes sense to me that they would want to know this.

BL: Oh, okay.

NL: There's something in front of me that looks like red dust. It's something about inhaling it. You inhale it sometimes, and that's giving me a state of mind, or calmness. I don't know what that is, exactly.

BL: Are you supposed to do everything that they [inaudible]?

NL: I think I feel restrained, but lucid at the same time. I don't feel combative. I don't feel like I care about cooperating or not. It's all okay with me. It's all okay with me, and it just makes sense. I know that there's somebody watching me out there. They're watching. I feel there's human military involved here, and this is important.

BL: Okay. So although it sounds like a couple of these, shall we say, people, there haven't seemed fully human, some of the other ones do seem entirely human. Is that correct?

NL: Yes. Some seem human and some only part, like the tall, white ones that were on the column. Now, there's a mixture here of a couple of different kinds.

BL: We're going to zoom ahead now and see if there's anything else in this experience that would be important for you to know.

NL: Somebody tapped me on the shoulder. He's touching me on the shoulder and telling me I did a good job, that person talking. They're going to see me again because I did a good job. He says this when I'm leaving the bubble and standing outside. This soldier looked like a man in a uniform wearing khaki. He seemed nice. He has a silver mustache. He's just a man.

BL: So, he's polite and decent?

NL: Oh, the other man that was in the bubble is going somewhere else. He doesn't come with me. He's going somewhere else. Maybe there is another ship that he's getting in.

BL: Okay, this man, when you are outside of the bubble has been commending you for having done very well.

NL: You know, this man I've seen before.

BL: The one with the silver mustache?

NL: This man I saw underground in one of my experiences. This guy gave me a chance. Wow. He gave me a chance in this underground when I saw the ship being made with all these scaffolds around it. They gave me a chance to participate because I kept swearing that I was ready, but I wasn't ready. I wasn't ready at all. Wow! And I was just swept out of that experience because I was too frightened.

BL: And when you said …?

NL: This man seems like the same man that I saw back then. He was in that room back then. That's at least a year ago.

BL: One year or so before this one?

NL: I ran away from them.

BL: You kept saying that you weren't ready for that.

NL: I was ready. I thought I was ready to participate, consciously, without having to be altered, in whatever was going on. And so I had an experience where I was conscious in the beginning, alert and awake. I saw everything, but I couldn't handle it, so I ran, and I freaked out so that I was subdued and returned. I was disappointed. I was so disappointed that I couldn't keep myself calm.

BL: I think that's understandable. But this time you are staying calm.

NL: Yes.

BL: But in this one, no harm's being done to you, apparently. Are they not physically examining you?

NL: I think they took some blood. I think they may have taken some blood before I came in and took my temperature. That's all.

BL: Okay. So nothing was particularly frightening. Is that right?

NL: Yes.

BL: Okay. Just notice now how it is that you get returned to your own home and your bed.

NL: I walked into my room. Somebody gave me something. A drug. Some kind of drug, or injection in the house, and walked me to my room and my bed.

BL: Okay. Was there any difficulty getting into your house or anything?

NL: We just walked in. I don't know where the dogs are. There must be a way to calm dogs down.

BL: Okay, so you're back in bed.

NL: Mm-hmm (affirmative). I'm tired. I think I got back around 3:30, 3:40. And I have to work in a couple of hours.

BL: Right. So you get up with the alarm, as usual.

NL: Mm-hmm (affirmative).

BL: Okay. Well, you've done very, well remembering the details of this experience, and you'll be able to continue to remember them. Right now, we need to come back to this time, and this place, and this situation, bringing back everything that you've just experienced, that you've just learned and any thoughts and any feelings that you have about that experience you will remember all those details. You've done well.

(End of Excerpt)

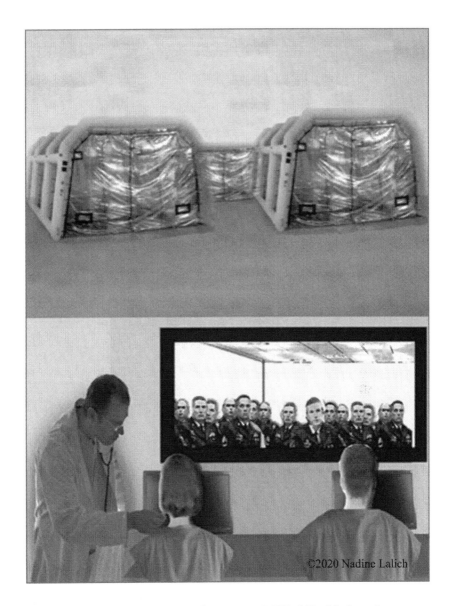

Interrogation in Underwater MILAB Abduction

11
FINDING RESOLUTION

It has been many years since I first became consciously aware of the paranormal experiences involving non-human entities that were happening in my life. Initially, the shock, confusion, and fear were so intense that to function in my daily life, I had to deny and bury my awareness persistently. Over time, my many journals filled to the brim with bizarre details, making it impossible for me to deny the extraordinary experiences. Hundreds of questions plagued me, and my fear slowly turned into resentment and anger. Eventually, it became impossible to pretend that nothing was happening. Although I can only speculate as to the genuine nature of these events, I strongly suspect there may be some truth to certain aspects of my experiences.

First, I believe that a small percentage of my experiences may have been actual physical encounters. Those encounters appeared to include physical, extraterrestrial biological entities that may originate from within our third-dimensional universe. At times, the physical experiences have also involved humans, alien-human hybrids, and cloned humans, sometimes working in a military capacity.

Another percentage of my experiences have not appeared to be physical, nor did they seem to take place in the third dimension as we know it. In those instances, I often felt quite lucid and consciously connected with intelligent beings, but it did not appear that my body was physically present! If humans do possess an etheric or astral body, as some people think is possible, could it be that advanced intelligence knows how to remove it from a physical body? If that is the case, could I have been transported into a different dimension, or did those contacts take place in the third dimension?

The remaining contacts I have had occurred more subliminally. They would begin with a strong feeling that I was being contacted, but without a sense that my consciousness or physical body would be removed to a different location. These interactions would interject into my mind while I was fully awake, or sometimes into a normal dream state when extraterrestrial activity would suddenly appear. My conscious recollection of these events has often been as detailed as the physical or astral experiences.

Not all of my experiences have been included in this book. I chose not to add those that were extremely brief and disjointed. I also omitted experiences that were recalled solely through hypnosis, without any conscious memory. There were several experiences that may or may not be related to the ET phenomena that I left out. Lastly, I omitted a few particularly frightening or sexual episodes that may have involved Reptilians.

After years of struggle, it was a relief when I was finally able to accept the ET phenomenon and integrate it into my ordinary life. Thankfully, the fear was replaced by an intense curiosity to learn and share more about the subject. Had I been given a choice, I would have preferred not to have these experiences. However, when I consider the big picture, my understanding of the spiritual realm and the nature of creation tells me that nothing happens randomly.

As an optimistic person, I try to make use of everything that comes my way. Therefore, I was determined to find something good or at least useful within this difficult challenge. Ultimately, accepting that intelligent life is abundant throughout the universe shifted my perceptions of the cosmos and enhanced my spiritual and philosophical growth.

We are a long way from understanding the UFO and extraterrestrial phenomenon; therefore, I feel no urgency to draw conclusions. Eventually, we will find the answers to our questions. In the meantime, I am content to live with an evolving hypothesis. Whatever the future may bring, I plan to use all that I learn about the alien phenomenon, the universe, and the nature of creation to enhance my life and help me to become a better cosmic citizen.

Monday May 3. 2004 11:40 PM

Dearest,

OK- so I will note it down—
the fact that the night before last I
again experienced the "alien" phenomena.
I "dreamed" they were coming - I tried
to hide in a sleeping area - bunk (on a
ship?) Of course they found me—
an alien "officer" dressed in a red suit
(disguise) one like I have never seen.
They told me I was one of a number
of humans who they have worked with
for 5 years- That a very big event
will happen in the not too distant

[May 3, 2004 - 1 of 3]

237

future - and we will be called upon to act as liasons between the aliens and humans. They told us that my psychic powers would accelerate and I sat next to a human whom I could hear talk without talking (telepathy) The man was about 60 and very upset and fretting about what was happening to him. I remember seeing a large number of ships (12 or more) up in the sky at night and many different types of ships. It led me to think that a variety of alien species

[May 3, 2004 - 2 of 3]

would be coming to the Earth. — Blah! How I hate this phenomena - whatever it is. Next night there was blood on my sheets + pillow case — I had a bloody nose in my sleep.

That's about it on that stupid subject.

[May 3, 2004 - 3 of 3]

I kept thinking - I'm here -
I'm really here. I'm awake.
This is really happening.
I remember insects - they find
us very ugly + we them.

I remember a female
with smaller eyes and
some hair on head like
fuzz short + thin color
looked at me curiously
and she was almost
pretty somehow. They

[August 1, 2004 - 10 of 11]

12/04

As to my commitment to dealing with the other phenomenon? There must be a way to incorporate it into my daily life. Perhaps by integrating it in my neurons with some soothing music — a new attitude, a perspective? I don't ever want to go to sleep in consciousness again.

IRIS
Human

ROBOTIC

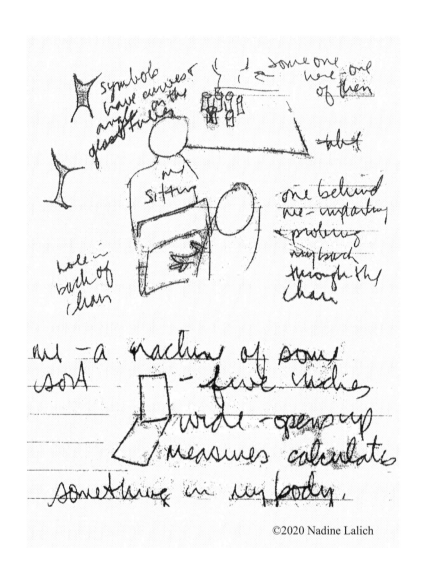

He says that we are the
focal points and that
God goes outward into
infinity that God
expands as
God we expand
Not to limit
my thinking. I said
I know

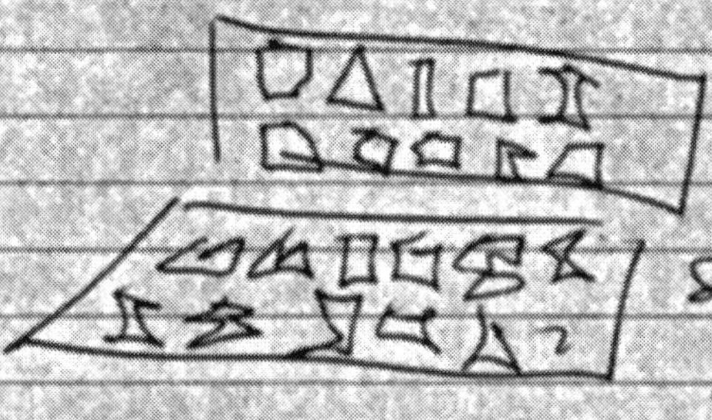

See through
Symbol
sheets

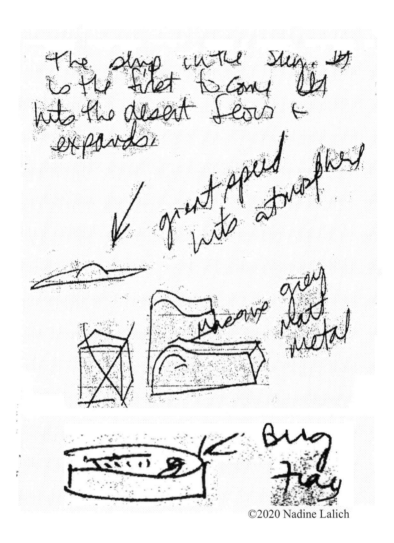

ABOUT THE AUTHOR

After a 30-year legal career working in civil litigation and public law, Nadine Lalich retired to focus on writing and art. Her studies include non-traditional healing methods using spiritual and meditative techniques, herbs, vitamins, and LED light therapy. She has experimented with sound, light, and sensory methods for subliminal programming, accelerated learning, and brain enhancement. A vegetarian and animal rights advocate, she also spends time in the study of psychology, quantum physics, and environmentalism.

Her years of first-hand experience with the UFO and alien abduction phenomenon led her to the study of Ufology. More about Nadine and her work can be found on her websites: https://www.alienexperiences.com, and at https://hbpublishing.net.

INDEX

Made in the USA
Columbia, SC
01 February 2020